Frederic Seebohm

**On International Reform**

Frederic Seebohm

**On International Reform**

ISBN/EAN: 9783337295158

Printed in Europe, USA, Canada, Australia, Japan

Cover: Foto ©Suzi / pixelio.de

More available books at **www.hansebooks.com**

ON

# INTERNATIONAL REFORM.

BY

FREDERIC SEEBOHM.

LONDON:
LONGMANS, GREEN, AND CO.
1871.

LONDON: PRINTED BY
SPOTTISWOODE AND CO., NEW-STREET SQUARE
AND PARLIAMENT STREET

# PREFACE.

This Essay was written during the American Civil War, and was in part printed at the time for private circulation only.

I have been induced to publish it at this juncture, in the hope that a calm statement of the economic argument in favour of International Reform may obtain an impartial hearing at a time when the public mind is in some danger of being drawn off the true scent by the cry for increased armaments and the abandonment of the principle of non-intervention.

I have added a Postscript on the relation of the reform advocated in the Essay to the policy of non-intervention so earnestly advocated by the late Mr. Cobden.

F. S.

Hitchin: *February* 1871.

# CONTENTS.

## PART I.

On the tendency of modern international society towards the increased interdependence of nations . *Page* 1

## PART II.

On the inadequacy of the present international system and in what it consists . . . . . *Page* 61

## PART III.

On the nature of the international reform required by the increasing interdependence of nations:

    1. In international law.
    2. In its interpretation.
    3. In its enforcement.      *Page* 95

Postscript on the relation of the reform advocated in this essay to the policy of non-intervention urged by the late Mr. Cobden . . . . . *Page* 143

# PART I.

ON THE TENDENCY OF MODERN INTERNATIONAL SOCIETY TOWARDS THE INCREASED INTERDEPENDENCE OF NATIONS.

# CHAPTER I.

I. ON THE LAWS OF NATURE REGULATING INTERNATIONAL SOCIETY.

PRACTICAL MEN shrink from having anything to do with whatever will not work.

Taught by experience, they have learned to recognise the existence of facts so firmly fixed in the constitution of things by nature, that for want of a clearer term we call them *laws of nature*. And all thinking men are agreed that nothing which clashes with these laws does or can work; while everything which does or will work must do so by using and obeying the laws of nature, by acting in concert with them, and in no wise against them.

This faith of practical men in the laws of nature, and utter distrust of everything which clashes, or is supposed to clash, with them, is not confined to the laws embraced in the physical sciences only. With increasing knowledge the current of modern thought has set in with increasing force in favour of entire and implicit faith in *all* laws of nature, including those embraced in political science.

As surely as the engineer knows that, unless he construct his bridge in accordance with the laws of mechanical science it will not stand, so surely does the merchant, in planning a trade transaction, or the Chancellor of the Exchequer, in framing a budget, know that the one or the other will succeed only so far as it is in strict accordance with the laws of political economy. Monopolies and protective duties, statutes of wages, and a hundred other things which were found to clash with these laws, have one after another been wisely swept away like cobwebs to the domain of the moles and bats.

Now, using the term 'laws of nature' in this sense strictly, and in no looser one, if it be really proved that such and such reforms are required to bring the present international system into harmony with the facts and laws of nature in points in which it now clashes with them, and consequently does not work, it will be seen at once that these reforms are required by something far more inexorable than the ' Lex Naturæ ' of the Jurists— that, in fact, they are steps in the great march of civilisation which, the world and the human race being constituted as they are, must inevitably be taken, unless we prefer that human progress should halt on its career.

## II. THE INTERDEPENDENCE OF NATIONS NOT OPTIONAL BUT BY LAW OF NATURE.

HAVING, in the previous section, clearly defined what we mean by laws of nature, the reader's attention is called to the fact that, as it is by law of nature, and not merely by human contrivance, that men are led to become socially connected and interdependent, so it is by law of nature, and not merely by human contrivance, that nations are led to maintain international intercourse and to become more or less dependent one on another.

Each country *might* have been endowed with a similar climate and soil. The air *might* have been made to fill only the valleys as the sea does now. In a thousand other ways each nation *might* have been made self-subsistent, and as effectually barred out from intercourse with every other as if each had been a separate world. But the world, *as it is*, with its arctic, temperate, and torrid zones, its varied soils and natural productions, its iron and coal beds lying in one zone, its cotton growing only in another—the world, *as it is*, with its nations of different habits and different races, separated by difference of language, but not cut off altogether the one from the other, because both capacity and inducement have been given, as they increase in knowledge and skill, more and more to bridge over the straits between them—the world, *as it is*, is so framed as, instead of keeping nations isolated and separate, to compel them, as they advance in civilisation, more and more to weave the web of intercourse—to entangle, as it were, the threads of their national prosperity into an international skein. Experience has taught us that if a nation choose to act selfishly and, by corn laws or anything else, unduly to check international intercourse and interchange of wealth, it will thereby inevitably lessen its own selfish share of the comforts of life. And clearly it is not merely by human contrivance, or by any human law, but by *law of nature* that it is so.

### III. ON THE LAWS BY WHICH THE DEGREE OF INTERNATIONAL DEPENDENCE IS DETERMINED.

BUT while all nations are by law of nature made more or less dependent upon international intercourse, obviously the degree in which they are dependent differs materially.

Nations may, in this respect, be regarded as roughly divisible into three groups or classes:

    1st. Those thinly peopled, exporting natural produce, and importing manufactures and luxuries.

    2nd. Those well peopled, consuming their own produce, and manufacturing their own goods.

3rd. Those densely peopled, exporting manufactures and luxuries, and importing natural produce.

And these three classes may be said to represent three stages in a nation's history.

Nations in their youth have almost always passed through the first or *youthful* stage ; many have passed from it into the second, or *self-subsistent* stage ; and a few pioneer nations have passed on through this middle stage into the third, or *most dependent* stage.

But it is not a matter of a nation's own choice altogether in which of these stages it shall permanently remain. This question also is determined, not merely by national will or the contrivance of governments, but by certain *laws of nature* ; under these laws nations are indeed free to take what course they may choose, but they cannot rid themselves of them. They may act in opposition to what by those laws is their own true interest, but whether they do so through ignorance or folly, it will be at the cost of abridged prosperity and often of actual suffering.

It is not denied that nations may continue in the self-subsistent stage for long periods of history *under certain peculiar circumstances.* But it is submitted that a careful review of the facts of modern history may enable us to point out with something of certainty what those peculiar circumstances are under which alone nations can remain for long in the self-subsistent stage of national life, and to judge whether those circumstances, as a matter of fact, do now or are likely in the future to exist.

Thus it may be regarded as a fact established by political economists, that unless a nation's *own economic condition* be such as to keep down its population within limits proportioned to the limits of its land, one of two results is certain to follow *sooner or later;* either it will have to suffer the miseries and hardships of over-population, or it will have to expand itself, and pass on into the third stage of national existence.

If it is to remain for long in the self-subsistent stage of national life, the prosperity and comfort of its people is dependent upon the existence of a powerful check upon the increase of population.

Now, putting aside the check which a very high moral condition and standard of comfort in a people would produce, as a thing which, however much to be desired and striven after, does not operate in any but the highest stages of civilisation; and looking at the facts of the case as they now are and for some time are likely to be, it appears to be established further that in a state of society in which men as they grow up can most readily marry and put themselves into a similar position to that of others around them—as when the whole population are detached from the land and work for weekly wages—population is most likely to increase rapidly, because there is the least check upon its increase.

But that in a state of society in which there are obstacles to early marriage, and men must wait till they have saved money or inherited the position of others before they can marry and place themselves in a similar position to those around them—as *e. g.* in a state of peasant proprietorship—population will remain most nearly stationary, because there will be the greatest check upon its increase.

Thus if the peasantry of a nation have emerged out of feudal serfdom into peasant proprietorship, and at the same time the proportion of town and trading population to the country population is small, you have a nation in which the population may well remain nearly stationary and the nation itself remain for a long period in the second or self-subsistent stage of national existence. While, should it have chanced that from any cause the proportion of town to country population is large, and at the same time the peasantry have not emerged out of feudal serfdom into peasant proprietorship, but have become detached from the soil and work at their own free will for weekly wages, you have a nation probably destined to increase rapidly in population, and which, if new channels of employment are not opened out as fast as population increases, will suffer the evils of overpopulation in all their force. If new channels of occupation are opened out as population increases, such a nation will quickly outgrow the limits of its land, and its prosperity will become more and more rapidly dependent upon free international intercourse. . In fact such a nation will be compelled to pass through the second stage into the third or most dependent one unless there be actual barriers against international intercourse strong enough to prevent it.

If there be effectual barriers against international intercourse, whatever their nature, nations will of course be forced at all costs to enter and remain in the self-subsistent state—suffering less or more according as the physical character of their country, and their own economic condition, favour a policy of self-subsistence or otherwise.

But inasmuch as these barriers, in the long run, *inflict suffering* and are *removable*, their removal is only a question of time. When the suffering is sufficiently keenly felt, nations will rise and break through them. They are not barriers placed by law of nature, irrevocably fixed—they are green withes which a Samson rising in his strength may shake off.

As a matter of fact these barriers are fast melting away. Commercial treaties and the spread of *Free Trade* doctrines are steadily doing their work.

And the result is that, as years roll on, the question of how long the great nations can continue in the *self-subsistent* stage of national life—of how soon they will be constrained to follow the steps of the pioneer nations into the *most dependent* stage—is becoming more and more an *economic* question for each nation to answer according to its own economic condition. And the future of nations in this respect is therefore becoming more and more dependent upon causes having their root often far back in the past and less and less within the range of a nation's present choice or control.

It is believed that the rapid, but not necessarily on that account superficial, review of the actual facts of modern economic history contained in the following chapter, will not only illustrate, so far as is needful for the present purpose, the correctness of these general principles, but also leave no doubt on the mind of the reader as to what, under existing laws of nature, is the actual and inevitable tendency of modern international society.

## CHAPTER II.

### I. INTRODUCTORY.

WHAT is the tendency of modern International Society ? Are civilised nations likely to plod on as most of them have done for the past five centuries in the self-subsistent state ? Or are they inevitably drifting towards a condition of greater and greater dependence on international intercourse ?

It has been stated that in proportion as the barriers to free international intercourse give way before increasing intelligence, the answer to this question is more and more to be sought rather in the economic condition of the nations themselves than in the direct intention and policy of their rulers.

It is accordingly proposed in this chapter to pass in review the economic history and condition of modern nations. And as it may be convenient to do so in the order of their present dependence on international commerce, it is proposed to take the case :

    1st. Of those nations which have already entered the '*most dependent*' stage of national life.

2nd. Of those in the '*self-subsistent*' stage; and
3rd. Of those in the '*youthful*' stage.

Taking the double test afforded, first, by the proportion of the annual exports and imports of a country to the number of its inhabitants; and secondly, by the proportion of its population to the extent of its territory, it will not be difficult to separate them with sufficient accuracy into three groups.

Relying on the valuable information contained in 'Puissance comparée des divers États de l'Europe, par Maurice Block, Gotha, 1862,' the following classification may fairly be adopted:

|  |  | Annual Value of Imports and Exports per head of the Population |  | Population per square Kilograme |
|---|---|---|---|---|
| Nations in the most dependent stage. | *Holland* | £12.8 | ... | 107 |
|  | *Great Britain* | 11.3 | ... | 93 |
|  | *Switzerland* | 10.0 | ... | 61 |
|  | *Belgium* | 7.3 | ... | 158 |

The above nations are dependent most years on foreign supplies of food.

|  |  |  |  |  |
|---|---|---|---|---|
| Nations in the self-subsistent stage. | France | ... | 4.2 | ... | 68 |
|  | Italy | ... | — | ... | 95 |
|  | Zollverein | ... | 3.4 | ... | 64 to 74 |
|  | Denmark | ... | 3.2 | ... | 44 |
|  | Greece | ... | 2. | ... | 22 |
|  | Sweden } Norway } | ... | 1.8? | ... | 7? |
|  | Spain | ... | 1.4 | ... | 31 |
|  | Austria | ... | 1.4 | ... | 54 |
|  | Portugal | ... | 0.9 | ... | 39 |
|  | Russia | ... | 0.8 | ... | 12 |
|  | Turkey | ... | ? | ... | 17 |

Nations in the youthful stage. { The United States; Brazil, and the South American Republics, British Colonies, &c., &c.

Finally, to these three groups or classes may be added another embracing the more or less *uncivilised* nations:

China, Japan, &c.,

which require some consideration, owing to the intimate connexion growing up between them and civilised nations.

### II. ON THE MOST DEPENDENT NATIONS GENERALLY—THEIR TENACITY OF LIFE.

CONFINING our attention at present to the most dependent nations, it may be well to make a few general remarks before passing to the consideration of the case of each nation in particular.

With respect to these nations, the great point to be ascertained will be *whether their dependence on international trade is likely to be permanent.*

It has often been remarked how precarious a foundation of *permanent* prosperity a dependence on international commerce has, in the course of history, proved itself to be. And many a lesson has been read to modern nations on this text. But it may well be questioned whether, text and context taken together, such really is the lesson to be learned from history. So far as I can gather the thread of its teaching, it is precisely the reverse. Tyre, Venice, Genoa, have doubtless left us the lesson of their fall. But the discovery of the passage round the Cape of Good Hope in itself affords too good a reason for a great decline of Mediterranean trade to make the case of these cities a representative one. Setting aside this exceptional case of the Mediterranean ports, the great fact to be learned from the commercial history of the past five centuries I conceive to be the *tenacity of life*, if I may so speak, exhibited by commerce and commercial peoples.

The fact that these very four nations, which now stand out as the most dependent on foreign commerce, were the very four nations of which (Mediterranean cities excepted) the same could probably have been said *five hundred years ago*, is itself a telling proof of this. And the fact that each of these nations retains now, in the nineteenth century, the distinctive commercial character by which it was marked in the fourteenth, is a further and still more telling proof. Thus, in the fourteenth century, Holland was mainly a *commercial* as distinguished from a manufacturing country, and it is so now. Belgium was mainly a *manufacturing* as distinguished from a commercial country, and it is so now. Switzerland was the *same*, and it is so now. England was marked by the combination of *both* commercial and manufacturing enterprize, and it is so now.

And again, if we take the case of the great maritime cities of the more self-subsistent countries, barring the exceptional cases alluded to, they certainly have exhibited a striking tenacity of life. The three surviving Hanse towns — Hamburg, Lubeck, and Bremen — were among the very earliest members of the Hanseatic League. Together with Rostock, Wismar, and Danzic, they were the chief commercial ports of North Germany five centuries ago, and they are so still. Marseilles was the chief commercial port of France, and Barcelona of Spain, in the Middle Ages, and they are so still.

Still further, there are districts in self-subsistent countries in which manufactures are now carried on. These are for the most part striking witnesses to that strange tenacity of life which has enabled germs of commerce, planted in unfavourable soil, to retain a struggling vitality through centuries of adverse circumstances. Take, for instance, the manufactures of France. The linen and woollen manufactures of the north, and the silk manufactures of the south-east, alike date back to the fourteenth century, or an earlier period. And again, those of Spain. Catalonia was the main manufacturing district of Spain in the fourteenth century, and, through all vicissitudes, it is so still. The woollen manufactures of Flanders spread under cover of the Hanseatic League, along the banks of the Rhine, and the Rhenish provinces are the great manufacturing district of Germany at the present moment.

But will the tenacity of life which has so marked the past history of commercial nations continue?

A very brief review of the causes which led most nations to adopt a self-subsistent policy, and the circumstances under which the most dependent nations in spite of these causes maintained their dependence on international commerce, will show clearly that present circumstances are at least far more favourable to its continuance than those of the past.

Modern international history may be said to date from the era when the idea of a '*nation*' became connected with the *country* inhabited by it. While the great waves of Teutonic emigration were one after another sweeping over Europe, the *nation* was the *tribe or people*, irrespective of its local home. The sovereign ruled over the *tribe or people* and aimed at universal dominion over all lands they might choose to overrun and conquer. Their very laws of tenure were such, it is said, as to compel those of the invading tribe who devoted themselves to agriculture, annually to shift about from one tract of land to another, in order to prevent their becoming rooted to the soil, and thus unfitted for their roaming conquering life. The old international idea of universal sovereignty was essentially a warlike idea. A chieftain's thirst for dominion was like the Indian's thirst for new hunting grounds and endless prey. But the western shores of the known world once reached and conquered, and a limit put to the indefinite extension of dominion, the conquerors themselves were put upon the defensive. If they would not themselves fall a prey to new waves of conquest, they must make a home of their newly conquered hunting ground, and keep it and till it for themselves. And the need of defence against foreign foes, not only ended in rooting the nations to the conquered country; it rooted also the people to the soil on which they individually dwelt. As in an age of perennial war and conquest the necessities of self-defence drove the *nations* to adopt a policy of self-subsistence, so in an age of feuds and private war the necessities of self-defence drove every little *Feudal knot of society* to become self-subsistent and independent of its neighbours. So the Feudal system became necessarily identified with the self-subsistent stage of national life. Each manor became a little self-subsistent state; organised for self-defence and self-support. And the nation composed of an aggregated mass of these self-subsistent atoms, itself became a nation organised for self-defence and self-support. It is obvious then that the Feudal policy of isolation and self-dependence *was not adopted because such was the bent of the national mind.* It was on the contrary clearly forced upon nations, as it were, *against the grain.* The national instinct of the nomad tribe for fresh fields of conquest had to give way before the necessities of self-defence. The national hatred of attachment to the soil and agricultural pursuits had to succumb before the necessities of self-support. And thus the over-ruling cause why most nations entered the self-subsistent stage of national life may be said to have been, the prevalence of *international anarchy and Lynch Law* which formed so effectual a barrier to international intercourse.

The result of this was that the great Feudal nations, thus driven down as it were by anarchy and Lynch Law into a self-subsistent state, left the few cities and districts which devoted themselves to commerce, to pursue at all risks, a practical *monopoly of international trade*.

A certain amount of trade will be carried on at all hazards, and at all times. There are some things with respect to which even the most self-subsistent nations cannot be self-subsistent.

The chief of these were in the Middle Ages:—

1st. Fish, an article which the religious creed of the times made indispensable, even to the most inland countries.

2nd. Manufactured cloths.

3rd. Foreign luxuries, for which there must always be a greater or less demand.

In all these particulars the most self-subsistent nations were, as a matter of fact, not in the main self-subsistent.

The fishing trade and maritime enterprise in general of North-Western Europe had, to a great extent, settled itself on the shores of the German

Ocean and the Baltic. The manufacture of woollen and other cloths, carried on to some extent in other countries and districts, had mainly fallen into the hands of Flemish weavers. And the trade in Eastern luxuries was very much monopolised by the cities of the Mediterranean. Thus while neighbouring nations were unnaturally settling down under Feudal auspices into the self-subsistent state, these portions of the European community were becoming more and more dependent on their commerce.

How did they maintain this dependence?

No doubt the very fact of the monopoly they enjoyed and the large profit they obtained in consequence, enabled them to run war risks and bear their losses, just as the prodigious profits of a successful attempt to run a blockade may cover several failures.

But the main cause of their great success was their attempt, by no means altogether fruitless, to curb the anarchy which reigned around them, and to establish some sort of law and order in its place. The commercial cities of the Baltic, North Germany, and Holland, attained this end by means of the *Hanseatic League*. Under its shelter, Flemish manufacturing towns attained the highest point of their prosperity. The Swiss preserved their independence and commercial prosperity by means of the *Helvetic Confederacy*. The commercial cities of the Mediterranean lessened the evils which they could not banish from their seas by adopting as a common code of maritime law the ' *Consolato del Mare.*'

But their monopoly, however well maintained, was sure to find itself at last between the horns of a dilemma. For first, the partial failure of these attempts to preserve international peace and order, whether on land or on the seas, left commerce still partially open to the disasters caused by piracy and war—history abundantly testifies to this. And secondly, the very success of their attempt— the international law and order, more or less maintained by their united efforts—itself broke the bars of their monopoly, removed the barriers to commerce, and opened the way for other nations to take their natural share of it.

The history of the most dependent nations, as will be seen more fully when we come to regard them separately, as a matter of fact, bears ample witness to the check and diminution they received from time to time, mainly from *these two causes*. Nothing but the tenacity of life to which we have alluded could have dragged them through.

Now I suppose it will not be denied that both these causes of harm and danger are, comparing past with present, much diminished. For first, international law and order is respected far more now than in the palmiest days of the *Hanseatic* league. And secondly, while the gradual removal of the barriers to free trade and intercourse is cutting away the last shreds of the old monopoly, the most dependent nations have no longer to fear but much to gain from its entire surrender.

Hence it is concluded as the result of this enquiry upon general grounds, that for the future nations have a better rather than a worse chance of permanently maintaining a course of dependence on international intercourse than they have had in the past. What then should deprive commerce and commercial peoples of that tenacity of life which has marked their history hitherto? Cotton famines and the like may cause distress and wounds which it may take years to cure, *and therefore it is beyond all doubt our duty to prevent if possible their recurrence;* but they who chuckle over Lancashire's disaster, and begin to chant the dirge of her prosperity, know little what they talk about! If the manufactures of Flanders, Switzerland, France, Spain, and the Rhine have survived five centuries of anarchy, shall British manufactures, under far more advantageous circumstances, now be permanently checked by the disasters of half as many years?

### III. THE ECONOMIC HISTORY OF ENGLAND.

In turning now to the separate consideration of the economic history and prospects of the ' most dependent' nations, it may be pardonable to take first the case of our own country.

With the establishment of the Feudal system, England, along with other nations, passed, to a great extent, into the *self-subsistent* state.

How did she get out of it?

There are few pages of international history which, if we could get at the facts, would be more instructive, than that which records the partial migration of the fishing trade and woollen manufacture from the Dutch to the British shores of the German ocean, the consequent partial decline of Flemish trade and manufactures, and the planting on English soil five centuries ago of the germ of that maritime enterprize and manufacturing skill which is the distinctive mark of the English nation at this day.

With regard to the fishing trade, something may be attributed to physical causes. The sea gradually encroached on the Dutch shore until at length it converted what was once an inland lake into the Zuyder Zee, and formed what was once part of the main land into the island of Walcheren. It gradually, meanwhile, receded from the English coast forming Yarmouth sands and port, where a bay had once washed inland between the two Roman stations of Burgh and Caister, almost as far as Norwich. And from whatever cause, in course of time, Yarmouth port became a great fishing station, much frequented by Dutch fishing and trading vessels, and ultimately possessing a large and rapidly increasing mercantile marine of its own. It is not perhaps generally known that, under these circumstances, the population of this fishing town had risen by the middle of the fourteenth century to a point which it had not passed four centuries after.

With regard to the woollen manufacture, the inundations on the Flemish coast had doubtless *something* to do with the migration of Flemish worsted weavers to those British ports with which their seamen were most familiar. A more potent cause, however, was to be found in the internal and international anarchy prevailing around them, notwithstanding the influence of the Hanseatic league.

This league did not wholly prevent internal dissensions, nor could it prevent nations, who had nothing to do with it, from going to war, or exercising belligerent rights.

Flemish manufacturers were greatly dependent on *English wool*, as Lancashire manufacturers are now dependent upon American cotton. Constant interruption of international intercourse, sometimes for years together, made this dependence of Flemish weavers upon the importation of the raw material from England hazardous in a high degree. Whenever it was the interest of England to do so, whether as a civil or a military measure, the exportation of English wool was taxed or prohibited altogether by the English Parliament. Flemish weavers were thus liable to suffer from a *wool famine*, as our Lancashire weavers are now suffering from a *cotton famine*. These facts, together with the existence of a strong and tolerably settled government in England, were sufficient to induce large numbers of Flemings to migrate with their looms across the German Ocean to the land from whence much of their supply of wool had hitherto been drawn. The consequence to England was that the towns of the Eastern Counties began to swarm with worsted weavers, and the manufacture of cloth, by degrees spreading into other districts, took permanent root on British soil, and became a recognised source of employment and wealth to the English town population.

It is not perhaps generally known that the result of this Flemish immigration and the internal migration from rural to manufacturing districts which followed as its natural consequence, was so marked that the population of the counties in which the woollen manufacture rooted itself increased with almost incredible rapidity. I believe it may be stated with safety that the counties of Suffolk, Norfolk, and Lincoln, and the East Riding of Yorkshire, contained as large or a larger population in 1347 than, after a lapse of five centuries, they did in 1847.

And this important and almost forgotten fact bore other fruits.

The stream of emigration from the rural to the manufacturing districts naturally bore with it *bond* as well as *free* men. It presented a kind of 'underground railroad,' somewhat analogous to that between slave and free states in America, for the fugitive serf who could prove residence in a free town for a year and a day was legally enfranchised, and beyond the reach of any fugitive slave law.

The weeding out by the dread pestilence of 1348–9 of perhaps two or three millions (out of five or six millions) of the English people struck another blow at the already undermined institution.

Leaving the number of British acres unreduced, but reducing the number of tillers of them perhaps by one-half, this deadly plague caused great scarcity of labour. The value of the serf, in other words, rose in the market, and, luckily for him, his pluck rose with his sense of power.

The towns had suffered as much or even more than the country. There was great scarcity of labour in the towns, and consequently the wages of labour rose to double or treble their former amounts. What a premium this on the further immigration of fugitive serfs! Landowners invoked the aid of Parliament. Statutes were passed reciting that 'a great part of the people had died of the pestilence,' and enacting that serfs and labourers should work for the same services and wages as if nothing had occurred. But what were Acts of Parliament in such a case? In their own recitals we read the history of half a century of constant strikes and risings of the serfs, maintained as strikes are now by systematic contributions, of wholesale immigration of fugitive serfs into the towns by connivance of the townsmen, and finally of the general rising in various parts of England, known as Wat Tyler's rebellion. The result of all this was that serfdom was once for all turned up by the roots and the vegetable phase of the serf's history ended for ever. That portion of the British population which hitherto had been rooted to the soil now became, like the free town population, by its own act, to a great extent *detached from the soil*, and dependent upon wages in return for free work done.

Nor was the freedom of the peasantry a onesided bargain. Serfs having claimed the right to do as they liked with their labour, landlords soon learned to do what they liked with their land. The depopulation of the pestilence had permanently reduced its market value for ordinary agricultural purposes. There were no longer hands enough, bond or free, to till the cultivated land of England as it had been tilled before. And therefore, because it required fewer hands and paid them better, landowners began very naturally to turn arable land by wholesale into sheep walks, and grow *wool* instead of corn. Because feeding sheep paid them better than feeding what villein-tenants still remained rooted to the soil, multitudes of these latter were from time to time uprooted, and, in modern phrase, '*ejected*' by the landlords to make room for sheep. Thus was the emancipation of the serfs, as it were, completed and sealed by the landlords. The result of these and other causes was the most important fact in English economic history, —*that the freedom of British serfs did not end in peasant proprietorship, as in most other Feudal countries. They carried no part of the land with them, as the Russian serfs are doing, but became a free, detached, and, so to speak, loose population, dependent upon whatsoever they could turn their hands to; and mainly upon wages for free work done.*\*

The social condition of Britain at the commencement of the Tudor period may be thus described:—

  1st. The population was not nearly so large as it had been 300 years before.

  2nd. The number of labourers employed in agriculture had certainly been greatly reduced; because a much larger proportion of the land than formerly was in pasture instead of under the plough.

  3rd. Although the towns were themselves but the shadows of what they had been before

---

\* I have, since the above was written, entered much more fully into the history of the causes which produced this effect, in articles contributed to the *Fortnightly Review*, on 'The Black Death' and 'The Land Question.'

the plague, the proportion of the town or trading population as compared with the agricultural population was probably very much greater than in most countries.

4th. The masses of the population, *both in town and country*, were becoming detached from the soil, hiring out their own labour in the open market, and dependent upon wages for free work done.

5th. At the same time there existed in England the germs of maritime enterprise and manufacturing skill.

In these few facts we have the key to the after history of the British nation.

Had the masses of the British peasantry emerged out of Feudal serfdom into a condition of peasant proprietorship, as, through gradual stages of tenancy-at-will, copyhold tenure, and so forth, *some* of them undoubtedly did,—had peasant proprietorship become the *rule* instead of the *exception*,—the history of the British nation would have been turned into another groove. A gradually increasing population, gradually bringing new land under cultivation, and increasing only as fast as improving agriculture would permit—the powerful check afforded by a system of peasant proprietorship keeping the population within limits proportioned to the limits of the land—the land itself, cut up into narrow patches like the land of France, producing, under garden cultivation, food enough to feed about as many millions as dwell upon it now; but those millions, instead of being pretty equally divided between town and country, scattered more evenly and densely over the whole land,—no Manchesters, and Birminghams, and Glasgows, with their tall chimneys and crowded nests of population to break the general monotony—such might have been the present condition of England had her early history been other than what it was.

But the facts being as they were,—the masses of the people being at the Tudor period, owing to facts in their past history, detached from the land and dependent upon daily wages, the proportion of town to country population being great and increasing, the germ of maritime and commercial enterprise being already implanted, the British nation was doomed as it were, by its social and economic condition, under the laws of political economy, to take the course which it did take—to increase rapidly in population, until at length it burst the narrow limits of its island home.

We see clear symptoms of the commencement of this rapid increase throughout the Tudor period—symptoms exactly the reverse of those which followed the depopulations of the pestilence of 1348-9 —*a steady fall in wages, and rise in the value of land.*

A race now fairly set in between the increase of population and the improvement and extension of agriculture. So long as more and more land could be brought under cultivation, the race might go on. But while it might last for centuries, it is clear that it could not last for ever. Population in the end must outrun agricultural extension, because the one was necessarily limited while the other was not.

This point in the nation's history was reached during the closing decades of the eighteenth century. The fact that the importation of corn then commenced on a large scale afforded an unmistakable waymark. The population had trebled since the Tudor period, and it became evident, that unless fresh means of subsistence could be found for the rapidly increasing population, or some great and effectual check put upon its increase, the evils and miseries of over-population must be encountered in all their force. That indeed would be an ill day for England when, like an overstocked rabbit-warren, the only escape from misery and want, to the remainder, would be the periodic thinning out of surplus population, by famine, pestilence, or war! But happily England was saved from so hard a fate by the ingenuity of a few of her sons. It is not too much to say that the discovery of the mode of smelting iron with coal instead of wood, of the cotton jenny, and of the steam engine, doubled the resources of the British nation, and allowed another ten millions to be added to the population without lessening the prosperity of the rest.

The great revolution brought about by these discoveries was not accomplished without the throes and struggles which accompany all great social revolutions. Transition periods are usually dark ones. The evil becomes deeper, and is more keenly felt on the eve of deliverance. The cure often aggravates the disease for awhile. The pressure of over-population was increased for the moment by the introduction of steam power and machinery. Hand-loom weavers waging a hard warfare against the competition not only of their fellows, but also of these new agents which were found to do their work cheaper than poor toiling hands could, did not witness very clearly to the nation's coming prosperity!

Population, as it always does, had taken a fresh spring from the development of new resources. An increasing demand for labour had increased both the supply of labourers and the ratio of their increase: and the result was that the adoption of that free trade policy which it is the economical *interest* of *all* nations to adopt, had become an absolute *necessity* to *England*. The old medieval policy, which would have cooped up a crowded population within this little sea-girt empire without giving free scope to its resources, could no longer stand against the wild and dangerous discontent its evils stirred up in the hearts of the caged millions. Chartism with its 'monster meetings,' incendiary fires, incessant strikes and riots, proved too clearly that the great pulse of the nation was beating in feverish excitement against the bars of its prison-house. The British nation was forced, willingly or unwillingly, to stretch out as it were its arms to other nations, and freely to draw from them in one way or another the needful means wherewith to maintain the prosperity of a people, whose numbers had far outgrown the limits of their little island home and were still rapidly increasing.

Thus from the fourteenth century downwards, the economic history of England has pursued its course to a very great extent not only without regard to the intentions or policy of successive governments, but directly in their teeth.

It was in the teeth of acts of Plantagenet parliaments that the English peasantry became free workers for wages instead of peasant proprietors. It was in the teeth of Tudor legislation that the still further detachment of the people from the soil was accomplished by the rage for sheep farming. It was in the teeth of modern corn laws that the population of England became dependent on foreign supplies of food. The freedom of the peasantry and the freedom of international commerce, were alike wrung out of reluctant governments. They bowed to necessity no doubt, but in neither case did they do so until they saw it was hopeless to resist.

And what is the result? Why surely this,—

that having been thus far carried along by a current which is bearing us still further in a course of dependence on international intercourse—a current, the force of which we cannot withstand, and the course of which it is impossible greatly to control—we must still further bend our policy whenever necessary to altered circumstances, instead of expecting unalterable laws to bend to our traditional policy.

And what are our altered circumstances? Plainly these,—we have, under the operation of the laws of political economy, passed, during the past half-century, fairly out of the self-subsistent stage of national life, and irrevocably entered upon a course of great and increasing dependence on international trade.

It is not only that a million or two of men, women, and children have become dependent on the cotton trade, and that this fact has placed us in the awkward predicament, that, although we annually spend upon our army and navy £25,000,000 sterling, the blockade of a few ports 3,000 miles away, *which we have no right to break*, inflicts almost as great an injury on us as the blockaded states. If this were the only instance of our dependence on international trade, it might be treated as an exceptional case, and it might be said with some truth that it would be an unsound policy to legislate for exceptional cases. But it is not so. The silk, on the wages earned in the manufacture of which some 250,000 of men, women, and children are directly dependent, is all imported, like cotton, from abroad. The same may be said of the hemp, upon which about 80,000 are alike dependent. No inconsiderable portion of the flax manufactured in Britain is imported from abroad, and upon this importation somewhere near 80,000 persons may be said to be dependent. The stoppage, by blockades or anything else, of the supply of these articles would be tantamount to stopping the wages—the bread fund—of these hundreds of thousands of honest workmen, just as the stoppage of the supply of cotton stops the wages of the cotton weavers.

More than this, the wages of the British manufacturing classes are dependent not only upon the regular importation of the raw material by the manufacture of which they earn their bread. They run a double risk. They are also liable to be stopped or abridged by the stoppage wholly or in part of our export trade to those countries which consume the manufactured article. Thus inasmuch as three-fourths if not four-fifths of the cotton goods we manufacture are exported to other countries; therefore, in addition to the *whole* bread fund of the million or two dependent upon the cotton trade being liable to be cut short by interruption of our trade with cotton-growing countries, three-fourths at least of that bread fund is *also* liable to be cut short by interruption of our trade with those foreign countries which *consume* our cotton goods. The interruption of our export trade means, in plain English, mills working half-time or standing altogether. And so in the woollen trade, if half our woollen manufactured goods are exported, then half the bread fund of the half million dependent on the manufacture runs the risk of stoppage or abridgment from the stoppage or abridgment of our export trade. If a million are dependent on the iron trade, half their bread-fund runs the same risk. So of the 100,000 dependent on the earthenware trade; and the 100,000 dependent on the tin trade. And so we might go on.

With so many millions of citizens (for these figures add up to millions) whose wages are more or less dependent upon the maintenance of peaceful international intercourse, we can hardly conceive of any war of long duration in any quarter of the globe which would not by throwing them out of employment rob thousands of their bread.

Nor is it the *occupation and wages* alone of so many millions of the British people that have become thus dependent upon foreign trade and liable to be cut off by the quarrels of other nations or our own.

During the seven years ending 1858 something like four millions, on the average, of the British nation were annually fed on foreign corn. The fact is clear enough—a considerable proportion *every* year, *and after a bad harvest a very large proportion of our food*, is imported from other countries, and without that foreign supply millions of our people must inevitably starve.

Imagine for a moment then what the effect must have been upon England if the war had been between America and some other nation who had blockaded both Northern and Southern ports. Undoubtedly, in addition to the present cotton famine we should have had *corn* at a famine price too; and, with corn at a famine price, how would the rest of England have been able to keep alive the half million cotton weavers in addition to their own poor?

And if we have of late imported more and more of corn from abroad, it seems generally admitted that we are likely to want *still larger supplies in future.*

' The nations of the West ' (observes a writer in the *Quarterly Review*) ' have gradually become less capable of supplying themselves with food. While thousands of mouths are added daily to the number to be fed, agriculture, with all its marvellous improvements and scientific appliances, is unable to keep pace with the progress of population. A few years ago England was able to feed her own people from the produce of her own fields ; she now buys grain to the annual value of more than £12,000,000, and it is probable that before many years have passed England and France together may be under the necessity of importing corn to the annual value of £40,000,000.' Again, the same writer speaks of 'the very probable diminution of cereal cultivation in England, in consequence of the preference now given by many farmers to the rearing of stock.' Owing to the character of her climate he argues that 'England is placed relatively under very disadvantageous conditions for the production of corn, while she need fear no rival in the raising of stock;' and concludes that 'a change in the present character of our husbandry, by laying down a larger proportion of land in artificial grasses, pasture, and green crops seems, therefore, highly probable.' (*Quarterly Review, July* 1863.)

There is yet another direction in which the dependence of England on free international intercourse has, during the past half-century, evinced itself.

The tendency of the free trade policy adopted by England has undoubtedly been to remove those harsh checks upon the increase of population which must otherwise have probably periodically thinned the too crowded ranks of a miserable and ill-conditioned people. The increase of employment resulting from a great export trade, and the abundance of food occasioned by the free importation of corn, have no doubt acted as a direct stimulus to the increase of population. Nor has it been an unhealthy stimulus by any means; for there is no virtue in a restraint for which there is no necessity, nor can we well find fault with an increase for which there is both demand and a fair provision.

Look at the facts.

The rate of increase during the last decennial period of the population of the United Kingdom was only ·6 per annum, owing to the actual diminution of the population of Ireland after the Irish famine. This may fairly be looked upon as an exceptional case. The rates of increase in the home population of England and Wales were:—

| | | |
|---|---|---|
| 1831–41 | . . | 1·4 per cent. per annum. |
| 1841–51 | . . | 1·3 „ „ |
| 1851–61 | . . | 1·2 „ „ |

During the same periods the emigration from the United Kingdom was as follows:—

| | | |
|---|---|---|
| 1831-41 | . . | 703,000 |
| 1841-51 | . . | 1,684,000 |
| 1851-61 | . . | 2,287,000 |

Thus during these thirty years the rate of increase has steadily diminished, while emigration has as steadily increased. During these thirty years 4,674,000 emigrants had left our shores. Between 1815 and 1860 the number of emigrants was more than 5,000,000.

We can hardly say that the state of society revealed by these figures is other than it ought to be. Whatever the peculiar advantages of a stationary state would be under other circumstances, it would surely be anything but the index of prosperity as things *are*. A condition of society in which, owing to its prosperity and the elasticity of its resources, the population is rapidly increasing, and in which the new generations, instead of hanging heavily on the resources of their parents, rapidly move off to other lands and rely upon their own, is surely under existing moral and economical circumstances a far more healthy one.

Yet these facts, though illustrating as they do the increased prosperity of our country, illustrate also very strongly the state of dependence upon international intercourse into which we have steadily drifted. What would have happened to England, we may well ask, had her five million emigrants and their descendants remained at home? Who can tell what a debt of gratitude we owe to America for affording the outlet she has done during the past half-century to at least three-fifths of our surplus population? What should we do for the future, if anything were to occur which should close the channels through which during the past ten years we have been pouring out emigrants at the rate of 228,000 per annum?

The importance of this source of relief to the population of the British Empire will at once be seen if we compare the annual number of emigrants with the annual increase in the home population between 1851 and 1861.

Average number of emigrants per annum from the United Kingdom . . . 228,000

Average annual increase in the home population of the United Kingdom . . 152,000

From this comparison it appears that the rate of annual increase of the population of the United Kingdom would have been much more than doubled had these emigrants remained at home. So dependent has England become upon an outlet to other nations for her surplus population!

Now had all this been foreseen and proposed before it came to pass, as a result to be obtained by a certain policy on the part of the government, would it not have been firmly opposed? Would it not have been urgently objected that to allow the people of these realms to increase so rapidly, relying upon *foreign* raw material for their employment, *foreign* markets for the disposal of their manufactures, *foreign* corn for their food, and an outlet to *foreign* lands for one or two hundred thousand per annum of surplus population, was to make the prosperity of the British nation dependent upon the maintenance of everlasting peace with all the world? Would not cautious statesmen have foretold that the first war would bring a nation pursuing such a policy to rack and ruin? Would not they have denounced it as a 'policy of political suicide'? Yet in fact we *have* embarked upon a policy which, to be successful, *does* require the maintenance of strict justice, peace, and order between nations. Under the irresistible guidance of economic laws, and in spite of some counter legislation, we have pursued this policy with marked success during half a century of all but unbroken peace; and now at length when its results have attained a magnitude which we never dreamed of, and which bear us on without the least chance of our being able to reverse our policy —*now we find that we have yet to solve the further problem, how that justice, peace, and order are to be maintained without resort to those commercial blockades and other usages of war which inflict such grievous injury upon even neutral nations.*

## IV. THE ECONOMIC HISTORY OF HOLLAND.

It will not be needful to dwell long upon the economic history and condition of Holland. The facts are too clear to admit of dispute.

The population of Holland is denser than the British population. Her imports and exports bear a larger proportion to the population than British imports and exports do. Her commerce is of far longer standing than British commerce; and it may be said with truth to be almost the only string to her bow. Her agriculture is not capable of indefinite extension, and she does not possess that mineral wealth which has fallen to the lot of other countries; consequently, Holland more than any other country is dependent upon foreign commerce for the prosperity, and even for the very subsistence, of her people. Her history presents the most remarkable instance upon record of national vitality under great natural reverses, and is a signal example of that *tenacity of life* to which we have alluded as an attribute of commercial peoples.

The Dutch, as a nation, never sank as did most European nations through Feudal auspices into the self-subsistent state. In the first ages of modern history we find them engrossing nearly the whole sea-fishery of Europe, and largely engaged in general international trade. Dutch trading cities were among the first to join the Hanseatic League, and also among the first to secede from it when they had grown strong enough to do without its protection.

In later times, the internal and international anarchy which ruled everywhere threw the chief part of the carrying trade of the civilised world into the hands of Dutch shipowners. During the 17th century it is estimated that the international trade of Holland was nearly as great as that of all the rest of Europe put together. She is said to have owned nearly half the whole shipping of Europe.

Then came her reverses:—

1st. As other nations diverted their energies from military to commercial enterprise, her *monopoly* gave way. She lost the unnatural advantage which she had hitherto enjoyed through their neglect.

2nd. Though her enormous commerce enabled

her to push to a successful issue her long struggle with Spain, yet the heavy taxation entailed thereby, and by her wars with England and France, proved more than her already declining commerce could easily support.

Holland, in consequence, lost that commercial ascendancy which she formerly enjoyed. Neither the French occupation nor the union with Belgium was conducive to her prosperity, and although a brighter day appears to have dawned with her separation from the latter, yet she probably never will regain the relative international position she has lost.

Notwithstanding, however, that her past commercial history may have exceeded in brightness her commercial prospects for the future, the fact remains that her foreign trade is greater in proportion to her population than the foreign trade of any other country.

To protect this commerce she expends more upon her army and navy, in proportion to her population, than any other countries, except England and France, in addition to bearing the burden of a debt larger in proportion than that of any other country except England. It is obvious also that any further decline in her trade, or decrease in her population, from emigration or otherwise, would greatly increase the burden of these annual charges.

In a word, it is clear that the future welfare of Holland, to a still greater extent even than that of England, is dependent on the general maintenance for the future of peaceful commercial intercourse between nations, and the avoidance on her own part of the expense which any future wars in her own defence must entail upon her.

## V. THE ECONOMIC HISTORY OF BELGIUM.

BELGIUM has been noted for her manufactures since the age of Charlemagne. If Holland affords the most remarkable instance upon record of tenacity of life in a *commercial* people, Belgium affords at least as remarkable an instance of tenacity of life in a *manufacturing* people. For eleven centuries at least Flemish manufacturing industry has held its course through all vicissitudes. This in itself is a remarkable fact. But what makes it doubly remarkable is the further fact that throughout these eleven hundred years—from the age of Charlemagne to the present moment—the main branch of the manufacture of Belgium has been dependent upon the importation of the raw material from abroad. Flemish weavers imported English and Spanish wool long before the Normans conquered England. At the present moment nearly all the wool manufactured in Belgium is imported from other countries.

But although the manufactures of Belgium have survived for so long a period, like the commerce of Holland they have suffered loss and diminution over and over again from international causes.

That portion of Flemish trade which was connected with the Mediterranean, and the overland route to India, of course declined with the decline of Venice and Genoa. This could not be helped. But, from first to last, the chief enemy of Flemish prosperity has been the constant unsettlement of international affairs. We have seen how much Flemish prosperity owed to the protection of the Hanseatic League. But we have also seen how England gained a share of the Flemish woollen manufacture, chiefly in consequence of those interruptions of international trade which the Hanseatic League was powerless to prevent. Her own internal condition moreover — the want of unity between her independent towns—left her an easy prey to foreign invasion. The death knell of Belgium was all but tolled when she passed under Spanish rule. Civil misrule and religious persecutions, together with the arbitrary stoppage of the Scheldt for a century, were causes adequate to produce the ruinous results which marked the period of Spanish dominion. If to these causes we add the fact that, during the century succeeding her release from the Spanish yoke, Belgium was to a great extent the battle-field of Europe, we shall have mentioned causes sufficient to account for the decline of her manufacturing industry.

In the meantime the decline of her manufacturing industry seems to have thrown her people upon their agricultural resources. And as, like their French neighbours, and from somewhat similar causes, Belgian peasants to a very large extent became proprietors of the soil, it was a natural consequence that the population of Belgium should not increase at a very rapid ratio.

The agricultural population between 1836 and 1855 had hardly increased at all. The figures were:—

    1836 . . 3,261,456
    1856 . . 3,348,189

The increase in twenty years was 86,733, or ·14 per cent. per annum.

But the town population had increased much more rapidly.

Under the influence of internal and international peace, the old manufacturing spirit has risen again into great and increasing activity. The development of the great mineral wealth of Belgium has also added largely to her industrial resources. Consequently during the period within which the agricultural population has very much remained stationary, the *town population has steadily increased.* The figures were:—

    1836 . 981,144
    1856 . 1,181,374

Shewing an increase of 200,230, or 1 per cent. per annum.

Thus the proportion of town and country population has been of late gradually changing, and as the town, or *rapidly increasing* element, has increased in relative importance, and the rural or *stationary* element relatively decreased, as a natural consequence the rate of increase of the *whole* population has steadily increased also.

The ratio of town to rural population was as under:—

|      |    |            |
|------|----|------------|
| 1836 | as | 31 to 100  |
| 1846 | as | 34 to 100  |
| 1856 | as | 35 to 100  |

The rate of increase in the total population was as under:—

| 1836-46 |         | ·22 per cent. per annum. |
| 1846-56 |         | ·63  ,, |
| 1856-60 | (about) | ·70  ,, |

The fact would seem to be, therefore, that the extension of Belgian industrial enterprise, and the consequent growth of her town population, are very rapidly removing that check which for a long period the system of peasant proprietorship imposed upon a population already more densely crowded within their narrow territory than that of any other European State.

And what is to stop this rapidly increasing increase? So long as in her mining and manufacturing enterprise there is a demand for labour and a provision for an increasing population, what can stop it?

As we have stated, Belgium was rather a *manufacturing* than a commercial or maritime nation ten centuries ago, and she is so still. As the King of the Belgians has himself declared, 'the genius of his people is for industrial pursuits at home rather than for a maritime enterprise.'

A nation without either a merchant or military marine must be peculiarly susceptible of injury from the quarrels of her neighbours; and Belgium is nearly in this position. She possesses no navy; and so insignificant is even her merchant marine that its tonnage, if multiplied tenfold, would not bear the same proportion to the value of her imports and exports that the tonnage of the British merchant marine bears to the value of British imports and exports.

To set against this, it may be said that she has the advantage of her perpetual neutrality being guaranteed by the great powers. Undoubtedly she has; but her peculiar political position, while sparing her the large military expenditure of nations who rely solely on their own power for their own defence, does not do anything to screen her from injuries inflicted by the quarrels of other nations upon neutral commerce.

She has, like England, to complain of 'great distress in some branches of industry' which the

American war and tariff '*have destroyed*' (Mr. Sandford to Mr. Seward, May 10th, 1861); and there can be little doubt that her future welfare is as much bound up as that of other nations in the solution of those international problems to which attention is called in these pages.

VI. THE ECONOMIC HISTORY OF SWITZERLAND.

The economic history of Switzerland presents considerable analogy to that of Belgium.

From the fourteenth century she has been distinguished, like Belgium, as a *manufacturing* rather than as a *commercial* nation.

In Switzerland, as in Belgium, agriculture has been carried on side by side with manufactures, by a hardy and thrifty race of peasant proprietors. Consequently two forces, so to speak, have been at work—the one tending to check the increase of population, the other tending to produce it. There is in fact in Switzerland, as in Belgium, an almost stationary agricultural population side by side with a rapidly increasing manufacturing population. Thus the rate of annual increase in the *manufacturing* Canton of Neufchatel, between 1850 and 1860, was 2·3, and in that of Geneva 2·9, while the rate of annual increase in the wholly *agricultural* Canton of the Grisons was only ·09, and in the Canton of Tessin, where there are special laws preventing the sub-division of estates, there was an actual *decrease*. If we divide the cantons roughly into two divisions, classing Appenzell (ex.), St. Gall, Thurgau, Zurich, Aargau, Basle, Geneva, and Neufchatel, as manufacturing cantons, and the remaining cantons as agricultural, the population and annual increase were as follows:—

*Manufacturing Cantons.*
Population in 1850   964,186
do.       1860  1,041,905

Increase        76,719 or ·8 per cent.

*Agricultural Cantons.*
Population in 1850  1,427,554
„        1860  1,468,589

Increase        41,035 or ·3 per cent.

These figures are sufficient to show how steadily, as in Belgium, the manufacturing, or increasing element is gaining ascendancy over the agricultural or stationary element of Swiss population.

Still further:—Switzerland like Belgium possesses no merchant marine of her own. She is dependent altogether upon neighbouring nations for the prosecution of her commerce, and inasmuch as owing to the peculiar character of her territory, she possesses very little corn-growing land, and has consequently to import nearly all the corn consumed by her people, it is evident to how great extent her prosperity is bound up with the peaceful maintenance of international intercourse, without needless interruption or risk of disturbance.

### VII. GENERAL RESULT AS TO THE 'MOST DEPENDENT' NATIONS.

To sum up the main results of this enquiry into the economic history and tendency of the most dependent class of nations:—

1st. Their past history exhibits strikingly the *tenacity of life* which has characterised their commerce and manufactures.

2nd. They have had to suffer greatly, owing to their dependence upon international intercourse, from its interruption at various times, although they have outlived these international storms.

3rd. They are clearly becoming more and more dependent upon international intercourse, and consequently liable to suffer more and more from its interruption in the future.

And, finally, these results appear to be the inevitable consequence, under the laws of nature, of facts in the past history of these nations, and therefore to be beyond their present control. The Governments of these nations cannot prevent this growing dependence of their people upon international intercourse any more than they can stop the rising tide. The current of international history will pursue its course in spite of any legislation of theirs. The web of international inter-dependence will become more and more delicate and intricate. Its separate threads will become more and more entangled together. The clumsy machinery of the present international system will become less and less adequate to meet the needs arising from these altered circumstances.

With whatever tenacity, therefore, our statesmen may cling to the traditions of the Foreign Office, and seek to maintain the international system as it is, it does not seem likely that circumstances and the Laws of Nature will be made to bend so as to comport themselves with its harsh methods and antiquated forms. And if circumstances and laws of nature cannot be made to bend to the international system, it is certain that the *International system will have to bend to them.*

## VIII. THE 'SELF-SUBSISTENT' NATIONS.—FRANCE.

IN turning from the 'most dependent' nations to consider the economic history and tendency of those which as yet have not fully emerged out of the 'self-subsistent' state, it will not be needful for our purpose that we should enter into a detailed examination of the case of each nation separately. But the case of France is so singular and at the same time so important, that it may be well to devote a separate section to its consideration.

France entered with England into the feudal and self-subsistent stage of national life. She also possessed linen, woollen, and silk manufactures of her own as early as the fourteenth century. The great plague of 1348 is stated, moreover, to have reduced by its terrible ravages the larger population of France in about the same proportion as it did the English population—a statement which, having evidence for the fact of the great depopulation in England, we cannot doubt was at least founded on fact. But the economic results of the plague do not appear to have been the same in France as in England. It does not appear to have had the intimate connexion with the emancipation of the serfs in France that it had in England. We read indeed of many charters of enfranchisement both before and after the plague; but nothing of any great emigration of freed or fugitive serfs from the country into the towns. Probably neither the prosperity of the towns, nor the extent of the manufactures, was sufficient to produce such a result. Those feudal serfs who were enfranchised by charter generally carried the ownership of the land with them, as the Russian serfs are now doing, instead of being detached from the land, as in the case of the English serfs. The French peasantry emerged, in fact, out of serfdom into a condition of *peasant proprietorship*.

And further, instead of the number of peasant proprietors *lessening* century after century as in

England, successive events have, in the course of French history, from time to time tended to *increase* the number. Thus, while in Tudor England landlords were ejecting peasants and yeomen and forming large grazing farms, in France the lands of the impoverished noblesse were passing into other hands and undergoing constant subdivision. And again, the religious persecutions, which drove the Huguenot silk-weavers out of France to swell the manufacturing population of England, not only lessened the proportion of the manufacturing population of France, but rooted still further her rural peasantry to the soil. For it is well known that they caused a still further subdivision of the landed estates. And lastly, the great French Revolution marked another era when the feudal peasantry of France became possessors of land. The result has been that in France there are five or six millions of landed proprietors. Of these about four millions may be fairly classed as peasant proprietors, and they are said to own about one-third of the whole soil of France.

At the same time, the long periods of civil and foreign war, the religious persecutions and political revolutions, which have marked her history, together with the absence of great mineral wealth, have kept back the town population of France to such an extent, that while in England the population is about equally divided between town and country, in France only one-fifth of the population appear to reside in towns of more than fifteen hundred inhabitants.

With four-fifths of the whole population *rural*, and the large majority of the rural families living on their own land in a condition of peasant proprietorship (that condition which of all others imposes the most effectual check upon population) France would appear to have inherited from her past history precisely that economic condition which would naturally tend to keep her population within limits proportioned to the limits of her land, and to keep the nation itself for a lengthened period in the self-subsistent stage of national life.

And what is the fact? France has accordingly until very recently had perhaps the most stationary population of any civilised nation except Austria and Portugal. The census of 1856 revealed the striking fact that during the previous five years the population had *hardly increased at all*.

But can even France, with all these economic causes in her favour, continue permanently in the self-subsistent stage of national life? It would appear that she cannot.

The census of 1856, while it revealed that her total population had hardly increased at all, revealed also that France presented no exception to the all but universal tendency of modern nations towards the preponderance of the town or increasing element as compared with the rural or stationary element in the population. It revealed the fact that while the *rural* population had been steadily *decreasing* the *town* population had been steadily *increasing*, chiefly owing to the emigration from the rural districts to the towns. If this state of things were to continue a point must be reached at length where the increasing element must gain a preponderance over the decreasing element, and the ratio of increase in the whole population increase with it.

The census of 1861 has indicated pretty clearly that this point has already been passed. During the five years succeeding the census of 1851 the total population was shown to have increased more than twice and nearly three times as rapidly as it did during the five years which preceded it.

Should economic laws continue to work unmolested by those frequent political vicissitudes which give so uncertain an element to French statistics, there can be little doubt therefore but that the population of France will increase in the future at an increasing ratio.

Already the value of her imports and exports bears a larger proportion to her population than is the case with the other self-subsistent nations, and with the exception of Italy her population is more dense probably than any of theirs.

Already about every other year France does not yield enough corn to feed her people, and she is dependent on foreign importations to supply the deficiency.

Already the wages of some half million of the French working-classes are said to be dependent upon the supply of American cotton, and at this moment they are sharing with us the miseries entailed by the American War.

Already Free trade doctrines are creeping into France, and commercial treaties are entered into with other countries, with the express object of breaking down the barriers which have hitherto unduly checked her international trade.

Already, in fact, France is *embarking*, to say the least of it, on a policy which must end in increased international dependence, and when once she has fairly weighed anchor and committed herself to the current, it is hard to see how she can ever return to the old feudal self-subsistent policy, which she has, until recently, so long endeavoured to pursue.

### IX. OTHER SELF-SUBSISTENT NATIONS.

With regard to other nations belonging to the self-subsistent class, it will be sufficient for our present purpose to make one or two general remarks.

1st. For the most part their experience proves no exception to the general rule that the town or commercial class in a country is the increasing one,—the agricultural, the stationary one. And consequently the tendency, so far as it goes, is *towards* the ascendancy of the commercial element, even in the case of these nations.

2nd. However long they may continue in the self-subsistent state, and however far they may lag behind in the race towards a greater and greater dependence on international trade, their condition and interests in these respects differ not in kind but only in degree, from those of the 'most dependent' nations. The peaceful prosecution of international trade is of great and increasing importance even to them, though it may not be the life and death question to them which it is to the 'most dependent' nations: even its temporary stoppage must injure them, though it may not inflict so dangerous a wound. And nations, like men, are in the habit of providing against less evils as well as against greater ones. They are careful to preserve and even increase their prosperity as well as to guard against ruin.

3rd. It may be remarked further, that although the same international causes may affect these nations *as nations* less severely than the 'more dependent' nations, yet from their peculiar geographical and political position, *those of their people who do devote themselves to commercial pursuits run a far greater risk of injury and even ruin than the commercial classes of the most dependent countries.* Wars and even the distant rumours of wars are often found to paralyse their trade; and this is in many cases the main reason why these nations are unnaturally kept still in the self-subsistent state, when, had they simply been left to follow their true interests, unchecked by political and international causes, they would ere this have passed into the more dependent stage of national life.

It does not therefore need further arguments to prove that the future prosperity even of the most self-subsistent nations is already, to some extent, and is becoming more and more, bound up with that of other nations, in the solution of those international problems to which attention is called in the following pages.

### X. NATIONS IN THE YOUTHFUL STAGE.

NATIONS passing through the 'youthful' stage are not, as a rule, dependent on international trade for the necessaries of life. But they are in a great degree dependent upon peaceful intercourse with other countries for their supply of luxuries and emigrants, as well as for the means of realising the value of that surplus of natural products in which consists their peculiar wealth.

# PART II.

## ON THE INADEQUACY OF THE PRESENT INTERNATIONAL SYSTEM AND IN WHAT IT CONSISTS.

# CHAPTER I.

### I. RESULTS OF THE PRECEDING ENQUIRY.

The results of the foregoing enquiry may be stated thus:—

1st. Two nations, Holland and England, fairly are launched as it were upon a course of dependence upon other nations, not only for luxuries, but even for the means of employment and the supply of food for their people.

2nd. Other European nations, by reason of the universally more rapid growth of their town as compared with their rural population, are more or less steadily tending towards the same goal. Some of them, especially France and Belgium, are already approaching the verge of the self-subsistent state, and are fast preparing to follow Holland and England into the dependent stage of national life.

3rd. Young countries, in all quarters of the globe, are rapidly rising by means of international intercourse in the scale of nations, and are dependent, as nations in this stage always are, upon the older nations rather for luxuries and emigrants —the means of enjoying and increasing their surplus wealth—than for the actual necessaries of life.

Combining these results into one wide view of the whole, we find the population of civilised Christendom rapidly increasing; we find it spreading over new lands where the raw products of the earth are more abundant. We find, in consequence, the necessaries of human life tending to become more abundant and cheaper, and a larger and larger proportion of the human race set at liberty, in consequence, for the contrivance and manufacture of the luxuries of life. We find these latter becoming more and more diffused amongst the masses of the people, and even wheedling their way into barbarous and half-civilised countries; and the consequence of this again is a growing mutual dependence springing up even between civilised and uncivilised nations. In a word, we find the system of division and co-operation of labour forcing its way into international as well as social society, economising for the benefit of all nations the labour and wealth of each—the several countries and peoples producing what the commonweal of nations most requires, and what they are best fitted and able to supply.

## II. MODERN MODES OF WARFARE ARE BECOMING INCREASINGLY INJURIOUS TO NEUTRALS, AND INCREASINGLY INEFFICIENT IN THE HANDS OF BELLIGERENTS.

Such being the economic history, condition, and tendencies of international society, it remains very briefly to point out the chief practical results which have followed, affecting the question immediately under discussion in this Essay.

They are two:—

1st. The practice of Modern Warfare is becoming more and more *injurious* to the interests of nations, and especially of neutrals.

2nd. It is at the same time becoming less and less *efficient*, as a means of attaining the ends of international justice, in the hands of belligerents.

Especially clear are these two facts, if we regard the question strictly from an *English* point of view.

England, as a maritime nation, has hitherto relied chiefly on her naval power. She has used her naval power in war chiefly in two ways:

1st. By destroying her enemies' ships, both merchant and others.

2nd. By blockading her enemies' ports.

It has been said again and again by the defendants of the *status quo*, that in the right of

England to do these two things, her naval power mainly consists. It is urged that if the first were taken away, our navy would have *nothing to prey upon*; if the second, it would have *nothing to do*; if both were abolished, our navy would be reduced very much into a naval fortification—a kind of national body-guard. The Prime Minister (Lord Palmerston) declared emphatically, in reply to Mr. Cobden, that to abolish these maritime rights would be to commit *political suicide*.

Two centuries ago these rights were far more effective and far less injurious than they are now. The right of capturing enemies' ships was at that time a most effective belligerent right to England, for while her naval supremacy was all but undisputed, the commerce of the world was, to a great extent, carried on by the commercial ships of *other* nations, and in time of war these were an easy prey. And while it was an effective weapon of warfare in her own hands, it was not a very injurious one when used by other nations against *her*. For not one-fourth of the commercial ships on the seas belonged to her—more than three-fourths belonged to other nations.[*]

But it is not so now. England is said to have as many merchant ships on the ocean as the rest of the world put together.

Now that all *ships* of belligerents are still liable to capture, while enemies' goods in neutral ships

---

[*] McCulloch's 'Commercial Dictionary,' under *Amsterdam*, 37.

are no longer liable to capture, it is plain that in case of our going to war higher rates of insurance would be charged on the cargoes of our ships as compared with those of neutral ones, and that this fact alone would in great measure cripple our shipping interest without a blow being struck. Our ships would probably either lie idle in our docks, be transferred into neutral hands, or pursue their wonted voyages with less paying cargoes and under risk of capture. A greater blow to our shipping interest than this could hardly be conceived.

And if the right of capturing enemies' ships is becoming more and more injurious to ourselves, it is also becoming less and less effective as a belligerent weapon in our hands as against other nations.

For if on the outbreak of war our enemies carry on (as they must do) their commerce in neutral ships, our navy will have no right to touch their commerce at all. Of what use then to us will this suicidal right be? Its effectiveness as a belligerent weapon is evidently gone. It is surely a pity that its power of injuring ourselves should be permitted to remain.

It certainly *looks* like a suicidal policy to persist in wearing a double-edged weapon, whose blunted edge is presented to our enemies and the sharp edge turned in against ourselves!

And the same may, to a great extent, be said

of the right of blockading an enemy's ports. It is easy to show that this also as a belligerent right has become more and more injurious to neutrals and less and less efficient as a warlike weapon to belligerents; and especially so in the case of England.

It is admitted by both opponents and defenders of what are called commercial blockades, that all nations except England are willing, nay anxious, that commercial blockades should be abolished; the advocates of their abolition urging the injury suffered by neutral nations from the practice.

The defenders of commercial blockades retort, that of course all other nations must delight in their abolition, because it would be tantamount to disarming England of the most powerful weapon whereby she has hitherto maintained her maritime supremacy.

It is somewhat strange, certainly, that the only nation anxious to keep up the right of blockading an enemy's coast should be England, the one nation (with the exception, perhaps, of Holland) which of all the nations of the earth would suffer most seriously from the blockade of the ports of other countries, and could not possibly survive for long a blockade of her own!

As was shown in a former chapter, England and Holland are many times more dependent upon foreign commerce than any other nation. To England and Holland alone of all nations would a strict blockade be absolutely and speedily ruinous. Other nations—Russia, Belgium, Austria, Prussia, the United States, and perhaps France—have within themselves more of the necessaries of life than they themselves require, and could, therefore, endure an endless blockade; but England and Holland cut off from foreign supplies of food must starve in a year or two, and suffer grievous privation and misery before even *many months* of isolation were over.

Finally, as the dependence of nations on international commerce increases, the injury inflicted by commercial blockades must obviously increase also.

And now as to the growing *inefficiency* of the right of blockade as a belligerent weapon. There are very few countries now *which can be blockaded.* The increased railway communication between nations has opened out many new channels whereby nations blockaded *on their shores* may yet carry on all needful commerce by *land* and through other nations' ports.

Again, that certainly is not an effective weapon which wounds the wielder of it more than the enemy upon whom the blow is struck. And yet in many cases the right of blockade must be so in the hands of England. For were England and the United States to go to war (which God forbid!) the blockade of the ports of the United States would cut off from her the supply of a *few luxuries*, while it would cut off from England both *corn and cotton* in the midst of the inevitable expenses and trials of a state of war! There can be no doubt that however destructive a weapon the right of blockade may be in certain cases, yet, against some nations at least, it is in our hands so inefficient, that in case of actual war we should be glad enough to let it lie idle in its scabbard.

It is not proposed here to discuss the different plans which have been suggested to prevent the injury to commerce which results from the exercise of these self-destructive belligerent rights. Suffice it to say that whatever plans have been proposed agree in attempting partially to *disarm* maritime war, and that the only argument of any weight raised against the principle involved in them is, that the more you *disarm* the more you *destroy the efficiency of war!* It is alleged that it is of no use to destroy the efficiency of war *so long as it is the only mode whereby nations can maintain their rights.*

And here the controversy rests. In the meantime we enter into commercial treaties, and become more and more dependent upon the maintenance of international peace and justice. We keep up a kind of see-saw between additional fortifications on the one hand and reduced military expenditure on the other hand, as the counsels of one or the other political party happen to prevail. Twenty-five millions of hard-earned money slip through our fingers each passing year to maintain a system acknowledged to be utterly powerless as a protection from the evils cast upon us by the quarrels of others, and becoming less and less effective as a means of promptly and justly settling our own.

## CHAPTER II.

### I. ON THE DISTINCTION BETWEEN LYNCH LAW AND POSITIVE LAW.

In proceeding now to the most important part of the argument contained in these pages—that part of it in which the gist of the whole of it may be said to lie—it is very needful that it should be guarded, at the onset, from doubt or confusion arising from the want of clearly understood terms.

It will readily be granted that there is a clear and marked distinction between a condition of society in which private individuals '*take the law into their own hands*' and '*do themselves justice*,' by resort to what in common language we call LYNCH LAW,* and a condition in which an efficient system of POSITIVE LAW is firmly established, by resort to which individuals obtain justice and maintain their rights.

Nor can it be denied that there is a distinction equally clear and marked between a condition of international society in which nations 'take the

---

\* '*Lynch Law.* Punishment inflicted by private individuals without the forms of law.' (Webster.)

law into their own hands' and 'do themselves justice' by resort to what may very fairly be called *International Lynch Law,* and a condition of international society in which the rights of nations are defined and guarded by a system of *Positive International Law.*

The analogy between civil and international society in this particular, as in others, may not be perfect throughout; but in all that constitutes the essence of Lynch Law on the one hand and Positive Law on the other hand, the prevalence of the one or the other, in international no less than in civil society, is a fact often witnessed and readily understood.

It is apprehended, *e.g.*, that no one will deny that the state of early feudal society in which *private* wars were carried on by feudal chieftains, was marked to that extent at least by the prevalence of Lynch Law.

'Because (writes Guizot) the system of *judicial* guarantees was vicious and powerless; because no one had faith therein, and cared not to have recourse to them; *in a word, in default of something better, men did themselves justice; they protected themselves.*' (*History of Civilisation,* iii. p. 179.)

That is to say, in default of an adequate legal judicial system they resorted to Lynch Law to maintain their rights. And so, I apprehend, it cannot any more be denied that a state of international society in which, in default of international positive law, nations 'did themselves justice' and protected themselves, would be a state of international society marked to that extent at least by the prevalence of what would be fairly called International Lynch Law.

And the analogy may be pushed one step further. The prevalence of a common code of morality or of commonly recognised rules of action tempering the harshness of private war between feudal chiefs would not in itself be considered as changing its radical character. So long as feudal chieftains continued, under that code of morality, to do themselves justice and take the law into their own hands, Lynch Law, it would still be said, prevailed, though to a less licentious extent and under a somewhat mitigated form.

It was so in fact, for (continues M. Guizot) 'Private warfare and judicial combat became established institutions, regulated according to fixed principles and with more minutely determined forms even than those of the pacific process. . . . . Men at this period had recourse to force: it was force which was to decide the question, but they desired to introduce into its judgment as much regularity, as much equity as it would allow of' (p. 182). And so, in international affairs, the mere fact that rules of international morality were commonly recognised by nations, and that war between nations had become an established institution, regulated according to fixed principles, would not change the radical character of International Lynch Law. If, having no other method of redressing their wrongs, nations had direct recourse to force, taking the law into their own hands and doing themselves justice, it would be Lynch Law which still decided international disputes, although nations might have tried to introduce into its practice as much regularity, as much equity as it would allow of.

Hence, though it may be a matter of question whether the term Lynch Law be an elegant or a classical term to apply to the practice of nations or of men 'taking the law into their own hands,' 'doing themselves justice,' and protecting themselves, in default of adequate legal and judicial institutions, it must, I think, be admitted that the term, if it applies to the case of the one, applies equally to the case of the other. In neither can the existence of commonly accepted rules of morality or of humanity tempering some of its harshness radically change the character of what in its essence is Lynch Law.

Such being the distinction in principle between Lynch Law and Positive Law, there remains the question of fact, how far International Lynch Law is still prevalent in international society; and how far it has in fact been supplanted by the institution of positive international law.

## II. THE ATTEMPT OF GROTIUS AND HIS FOLLOWERS TO REFORM INTERNATIONAL MORALITY.

IN a former chapter it was pointed out that modern international history dates from the establishment of the modern idea of a *nation*—from the period when the idea of universal dominion gave place to that of territorial sovereignty, and nations became attached, as it were, to the countries inhabited by them.

It will readily be seen that so long as any trace of the old idea of universal dominion lingered in the minds of nations or their rulers, international relations must of necessity have been so inextricably entangled and confused, the asserted rights of one nation so utterly inconsistent with the rights of every other, that anything like an organised international system was impossible.

While princes laid fanciful claim to one another's thrones, and formed and broke off alliances simply when it suited their own selfish schemes, no matter how many solemn treaties were thereby broken or how much unjust injury inflicted, Lynch Law was not only the only law actually in force between nations, but also the only law possible.

Any adequate examination into the state of international affairs during the 16th century—the age immediately preceding that of Grotius—would make it clear at once that European nations had by no means emerged fully from the transition period of international history. It would show that while, on the one hand, their idea of sovereignty nominally was the modern territorial idea, yet in practice they aimed at something much more extended and indefinite than any mere sovereignty over their own immediate kingdom.

And whatever improvement may have taken place in the interval, the unbridled extent to which Lynch Law was carried in the age of Grotius—the founder of the present international system—was, he tells us himself, the evil to correct which he wrote his treatise *De Jure Belli ac Pacis*. It was one of the 'weighty reasons' why he wrote it. 'I observed (he writes) throughout the Christian world a licentiousness in regard to war which even barbarous nations ought to be ashamed of: a running to arms upon very frivolous or rather no occasions, which being once taken up there remained no longer any reverence for right either divine or human, just as if from that time men were authorised and firmly resolved to commit all manner of crimes without restraint.' (*Preliminary Discourse, De Jur. Bel. ac Pac.*)

He clearly saw that it was by law of nature (and that in the proper sense as we have defined it) that men were driven to form social relations. 'The Author of nature was pleased (he says) that every man in particular should be weak of himself, and in want of many things necessary for living commodiously to the end that we might more eagerly affect Society.'

He saw clearly, also, that owing to this interdependence of individuals, no social community can be preserved, not even a society of *Robbers*, without some respect for justice and right. And he saw, too, that the same principle applied to the intercourse as well of nations as of men. The necessity of the practice of justice between citizens is visible (he said) to all; 'but great States that seem to have within themselves all things necessary for their defence and well-being, do not (he continues) seem to some to stand in need of that virtue.'

But although, as we have pointed out, the nations were passing through the self-subsistent stage of national life, yet Grotius could see clearly enough that, nevertheless, ' there is no State so strong or well-provided but what may sometimes stand in need of foreign assistance, either in the business of commerce or to repel the joint forces of confederated nations.'

And from this he argued consistently that 'if there is no community which can be preserved without some sort of right, as Aristotle proved by that remarkable instance of robbers, certainly the society of mankind or of several nations cannot be without it.'

Starting, then, from the fact that there existed only to a very partial extent indeed any system of positive international law, he proceeded, in the first place, to lay down what, upon that assumption and under those circumstances, nations were bound in natural justice to do and leave undone in their intercourse with one another.

'The leading object of Grotius and of his immediate disciples and successors (writes Wheaton) in the science of which he was the founder seems to have been—1st, to lay down those rules of justice which would be binding on men living in a social state, independently of any positive laws of human institution, or, as it is commonly expressed, living together in a state of nature; and 2nd, to apply those rules, under the name of *Natural Law*, to the mutual relations of separate communities living in a similar state with respect to each other.' (*Wheaton*, I. p. 33.)

Vattel also rested upon this fundamental principle the rules of international natural justice and morality which it was his chief aim to promulgate.

'Nations,' he says, 'being composed of men naturally free and independent, and who, before the establishment of civil societies, lived together in a state of nature,—nations, or sovereign states, are to be considered as so many free persons living together in the state of nature.'

And he thus expresses the object of his book :—
'In this treatise it will appear in what manner *States*, as such, *ought* to regulate all their actions.'

It will be seen, therefore, that those rules and maxims of natural justice which Grotius and his followers promulgated as binding upon nations *in foro conscientiæ* were in reality far more a code of international *morality* than of international *law*, in the commonly received meaning of the term law.

Nor did Grotius or Vattel confuse the system of morality which it was their chief aim to promulgate, with—what they recognised as a distinct thing altogether—a system of *positive* law. We shall see this perfectly clearly when we come to speak more fully of their views with reference to the latter.

Nor do even those who still cling to the phrase *international law* as applied to what are merely rules of international morality deny the existence of the radical distinction between them and the enactments of positive law.

It does not therefore seem necessary to bring forward any further authorities in support of an opinion which, when fairly looked into, can hardly be disputed.

It will be seen that in the preceding pages I have purposely given the object and opinions of Grotius and others in the words of Wheaton, so that the reader may judge for himself whether I have unconsciously misrepresented them to suit the purposes of my argument. It is fair, however, to say that in the paragraph in which Dr. Phillimore alludes to this subject, he argues that the rules of international morality are in a sense international laws. But if I mistake not, the evident dislike of the Doctor to the term international morality, and the reasons why he thinks it of importance to maintain the use of the term 'international law' for what he does not deny is merely *moral doctrine*, must, in itself, tend to support the view urged in this chapter.

The modern international system grew up while the nations were still passing through the self-subsistent stage of national life, when as yet the need had not arisen, or was not felt, for a complete system of positive international law. A thorough reform of international morality was in their day the pressing need of international society, and this reformation was the great work which Grotius and his successors attempted, and as a matter of fact have in great measure accomplished.

III. GROTIUS AND HIS FOLLOWERS ADMITTED THE EXISTENCE AND NECESSITY OF 'POSITIVE' INTERNATIONAL LAW.

It has been seen that the great work which Grotius proposed to himself, and so successfully achieved, was the promulgation of sound rules of international morality.

But did Grotius mean that international reform should stop with the attainment of this object?

Was there never to be any *positive law* between nations, practically regulating international action, in accordance with the general principles of international morality?

Puffendorf seems to have thought that positive law would be out of place between nations. Speaking of the rules of international intercourse observed by *tacit consent* among civilised nations—the only approach to positive law which existed in his day—he remarks:—

'If one engaged in a lawful war shall neglect them and profess that he will not be bound by such restraints, provided that what is contrary to them may be rightly done according to the law of nature [*i.e.* natural justice], he is guilty of no other sin but a sort of unskilfulness in not adjusting his proceedings to the nice models of those who reckon war in the number of the liberal studies, as a gladiator is accused of inexpertness when he wounds his antagonist otherwise than by rules of art. Whoever, therefore, wages war in a just cause may slight these formalities at pleasure, and govern himself purely by law of nature. . . Nor have those men any good reason of complaint who censure this doctrine as a notion by which the security, the interest, and the safety of nations are robbed of their surest guards and defence. . . The observance of the law of nature affords them a much more sacred support—one which whilst they enjoy they have little need of inferior methods of protection.' (*Puffendorf*, bk. II. c. iii. s. 23; p. 151.)

Puffendorf thus clearly denies not only the existence, but also the need, of any positive international laws. The laws of national justice—*i.e.* of international morality—he held to be the only and sufficient rule of international action. Positive international laws would be an 'inferior method of protection.'

But not so Grotius. In an age when there were hardly any positive laws of nations clearly defined and in force, he clearly asserted their existence and the need of their existence. He distinguished, more or less clearly, between the rules of international morality (*jus naturæ*) and what he called *laws of nations* (*jus gentium*).

'Grotius (writes Wheaton) considers the *law of nations* as a *positive institution*, deriving its authority from the *positive consent of all or the greater part of nations*, which he supposes to be united in a social compact for the purpose.'

And again, 'Grotius states that the *jus gentium* acquires its obligatory force from the positive consent of all nations, or at least of several.'

Thus, then, the laws of international morality—of natural justice—which he wrote his book to define and promulgate, were not in themselves, in his view, positive 'laws of nations,' unless or until they were adopted by the express or implied consent of most civilised nations. Where rules of international conduct were thus adopted, he considered that they became, as between those nations, *positive laws*, whether they were consistent or not with the laws of natural justice. In some instances some nations recognised different positive laws of this kind from those recognised by others, and it was evidently his desire, in promulgating sound views of natural justice, so to influence the usages of civilised nations as to make them comport with his own sound views, and so in the long run to mould thereby the positive law of nations which the common usage of nations creates.

Bynkershoek, rejecting the view of Puffendorf, also held with Grotius that the *usage* of nations was the basis of the *law of nations*.

In a passage quoted by Wheaton, he says that ' the law of nations is that which is observed in accordance with the light of reason between nations, if not among all, at least certainly among the greater part, and those the most civilised.'

And so also Vattel, in speaking of the positive law of nations, expresses himself thus:—

' When a custom or usage is *generally* established, either between all the civilised nations of the world, or only between those of a certain continent, as of Europe for example, or between those who have a more frequent intercourse with one another ; if that custom is in its own nature indifferent, and much more if it be useful and reasonable, it becomes obligatory on the nations in question, who are considered as having given their consent to it, and are bound to observe it towards each other as long as they have not expressly declared their resolution of not observing it in future.' (*Vattel*, lxv.)

And he remarks further that the *positive laws of nations*—i.e. those laws which proceed from the will of nations—are of three kinds: ' the *voluntary*, from their presumed consent; the *conventional*, from an express consent; and the *customary*, from tacit consent.'

And he concludes his remarks by laying down the rule that while nations, in examining what is their own duty, should consult the laws of natural justice which are always obligatory in the conscience, in examining what they may *demand of other nations* they should consult the *positive law of nations*.

Finally, Wheaton adds his own authority to that of the earlier jurists in the following words:—' The international law of Christendom began to be fixed about the time of Grotius, when the combined influence of religion, chivalry, the feudal system, and commercial and literary intercourse had blended together the nations of Europe into one great family. This law does not merely consist of the principles of natural justice applied to the conduct of States considered as moral beings. It may, indeed, have a remote foundation of this sort, but the immediate visible basis on which the public law of Europe, and of the American nations which have sprung from the European stock, has been erected, are the customs, usages, and conventions observed by that portion of the human race in their mutual intercourse.' (*Wheaton*, I. 51.)

We arrive, therefore, at the clear result that international jurists, from Grotius to Wheaton, have, with but few exceptions, made a more or less clear distinction between the rules of natural justice or of international morality on the one hand, and *positive international law* on the other. The former they called the law of nature, the latter the law of nations.

They granted, therefore, in principle the necessity of positive international law, and themselves aimed at the correction and extension of whatever of positive international law existed in their own times.

IV. WHAT POSITIVE INTERNATIONAL LAW EXISTS IS VERY INADEQUATE, AND INTERNATIONAL LYNCH LAW STILL PREVAILS.

While thus the greatest international authorities may be cited in support of the necessity of positive international law, and its partial existence in their times as well as in our own, yet we must by no means jump to the conclusion that because of the partial existence of positive international law, the prevalence of international Lynch Law has been practically put an end to.

It remains to be shown whether it is so fully established as really to supersede the resort on the part of nations to *Lynch Law*,—as really to make it no longer needful for nations ' to take the law into their own hands and do themselves justice.' And again it requires consideration whether much of what is really established usage on the part of nations be not analogous to those usages by which private war was in feudal times regulated and its harshness in some measure tempered, rather than to what ought to be regarded as really *positive law*.

In the first place, with some marked exceptions such as the declaration of the slave trade to be piracy, and the declaration of Paris of 1856, to both of which the express positive consent of all nations bound thereby has been solemnly given, it may well be questioned whether the rules of international action be sufficiently clearly defined to admit of their being regarded as to the full extent at least *positive laws*.

In the second place, the absence of any judicial or authoritative mode of interpreting these consuetudinary laws of nations gives them a vagueness which at once distinguishes them from the unwritten law of civil society. The common law of England, *e.g.*, is for the most part clearly defined by judicial precedent. which giving the positive sanction of the State to the point of law decided, from time to time supplies almost as fully as would special enactment the *positive* element which characterises the common law of England.

In the third place, however fully they may be thought by some to possess the characteristics of positive law, they are analogous to the maxims by which private war was regulated in feudal times in this essential particular, that instead of providing a legal and judicial substitute for Lynch Law, *i.e.* for the system of each nation 'doing itself justice and taking the law into its own hands,' they rather organise this system and seek to introduce into its practice ' as much equity as it will admit of.'

Under these laws what is in fact international *private war* has become an institution regulated by fixed principles, just as much as feudal private war did ages ago, instead of it being superseded by *legal and judicial institutions.*

Hence, therefore, the most that can be said of a large portion of international law—whether, strictly speaking, *positive law* or not—is that, like the old feudal code of private war, it tends to temper the harshness of Lynch Law without superseding its practice.

And lastly, even with regard to the declaration of Paris itself, so far as there exists no other method of interpretation but that of each nation judging for itself what it means, and so far as there exists no other method of enforcing it but that of each nation taking the law into its own hands and doing itself justice by its own military and naval power —so far Lynch Law still in our own times prevails between nations; causing cotton famines, destroying peaceful commerce, and thereby robbing thousands and hundreds of thousands, and it may be millions, of innocent citizens of even neutral nations of the wages on which they are dependent for their daily bread!

This is what, I trust, the terrible evils of the present war will startle the British public into seeing; for look at it as we will, I cannot see a single loophole through which we can escape from the most unpalatable truth.

The American War will not have been an unmixed evil if it open our eyes to the injury which the pursuit of right by the harsh methods of international Lynch Law inflicts, and is always likely to inflict, upon friend and foe alike; and especially if at the same time it force us to recognise the utter inadequacy of those methods, even with all the refinements of modern warfare, as means of promptly bringing to a just or an unjust conclusion an international dispute.

Were the power all on one side, no doubt it might seem to be otherwise. In such a case, a dispute may be forced to a conclusion at any moment by the nation whose brute force is superior. The weaker Power, whether in the right or the wrong, will yield, though it may be under protest. But no end of justice is gained. The dispute has not been finally settled. The embers may smoulder for awhile, but it is only to break out again, when further fuel is added, into a far stronger flame.

The inadequacy of the present international system lies therefore, it is clear, in a far more radical defect than can be reformed by any mere alteration of the rules of maritime warfare. It has been proposed to abolish those usages of war which are most injurious to neutral nations. The only strong argument which has been relied on against this reform rests on the fact that, to disarm war of its most disastrous and dangerous weapons, would be to make it a still less efficient means of obtaining redress for international wrongs than it is, and to render it a pastime which, in the words of Lord Palmerston, might be 'indulged in for ever without coming to any result.'

It is, in truth, inadequate enough already, and its inadequacy lies in the fact that Lynch Law never is, nor can be, an adequate means for the attainment of the ends of justice in a complicated state of international or any other society.

No reformation of the practice of international Lynch Law can, therefore, solve the international problem upon the solution of which the common weal of nations is becoming more and more dependent.

As was remarked at the outset, the problem is a double one.

The present system of international Lynch Law is both inadequate as a mode of obtaining international justice, and also injurious to other nations.

The international problem requiring solution is how to provide a more adequate security for international justice which shall at the same time be less injurious to the interests of nations.

In short, it may be possible to make the practice of international Lynch Law *either* less injurious to neutral nations *or* more effective in the hands of belligerent nations; but to make it both a harmless and an effective means of attaining the ends of international justice is a task transcending human skill.

V. THE INTERNATIONAL REFORM NOW REQUIRED IS THE SUBSTITUTION OF A LEGAL AND JUDICIAL SYSTEM FOR INTERNATIONAL LYNCH LAW.

In a previous section the fact was pointed out that modern international jurists deduced their international maxims by analogy from the principles which would prevail between individuals in the analogous stage of social society, *i.e.* in the absence of organised civil and judicial institutions.

I wish now to press the analogy between social and international life a little further.

Since the time of Grotius the ages have rolled on, the shadow on the international dial has advanced ; the state of international society is no longer analogous to a state of civil society without civil and judicial institutions, but to one more advanced. International society has passed since the age of Grotius into another and more advanced stage, and it is therefore necessary to compare with it a corresponding and more advanced stage of civil society, if we wish to draw the true present analogy between the two.

It will readily be admitted that a state of society which is marked by the absence of a civil and judicial system, or, in other words, by the prevalence of Lynch Law between men, is only a very temporary stage of the life of a civilised nation.

And what is that point in social history at which the system of Lynch Law breaks down, and the necessity for a civil and judicial system to take its place, becomes obvious and pressing?

Surely it is that in which it is found in practice that the resort to Lynch Law is not only a very burdensome and inefficient remedy to the aggrieved party, but also *hazardous to the lives and interests of others.*

When population is thinly scattered, and men have little or no communication with any but their distant next-door neighbours, they may wear their swords and fight out their quarrels in a summary manner without much danger to others. But were two citizens to fight out their quarrel in the crowded market, to the danger and actual damage of peaceable passers-by, it would be evident enough that some more harmless mode of settling the disputes of citizens than this must be provided.

## Inadequacy of the Present System. 93

We see in our own past history how, as the towns increased in population, and more and more citizens became dependent upon the peaceful prosecution of internal trade, the necessity arose for the general disarmament of citizens which has been so completely effected. And we see in the growth of modern colonies the same necessity arise, whether it be in the gold diggings of California, Australia, or British Columbia. The scum of civilised population collects in a whirlpool of excitement, Lynch Law for a while prevails. But this stage of colonial history is of short duration; with the increased population, a civil government arises, and the district which before contained only a handful of independent inhabitants, becomes, by the force of moral gravitation, a civilised state.

As we analyse the present state of international society, we find what is neither more nor less than the practice of international Lynch Law still to a great extent prevailing between nations, closely resembling in practice, and altogether identical in principle, with the state of Lynch Law which in a barbarous stage of society subsisted between individuals. We find, further, that as Lynch Law between individuals has always and everywhere been found to be inimical to private trade, so is international Lynch Law now found, as the Hanse Towns found it eight hundred years ago, to be inimical to international commerce. To carry the analogy one step further, it is submitted, that as the growth of commercial enterprise, and the consequent complication of individual rights and relations necessitated the gradual substitution of civil law and a judicial system between individuals, so must the growth of international commerce and the consequent complication of international rights and relations eventually necessitate the gradual substitution of *positive international law* and *an essentially judicial system* between nations.

Analogies cannot, I am perfectly aware, be pushed too far. It does not follow, in the least, that the law and the judicial system should be of the same type in the one case as in the other; it does not follow, in the least, that the change will be brought about by the same steps or the same means; but I trust I shall be able to show that, being necessary, it is not Utopian to aim at its gradual accomplishment, and that some tentative steps have already been taken in the right direction.

# PART III.

ON THE NATURE OF THE INTERNATIONAL REFORM REQUIRED BY THE INCREASING INTERDEPENDENCE OF NATIONS:—

I.—IN INTERNATIONAL LAW.
II.—IN ITS INTERPRETATION.
III.—IN ITS ENFORCEMENT.

## CHAPTER I.

#### INTRODUCTORY—THE THREE BRANCHES OF THE SUBJECT.

In proceeding now to discuss more fully the nature of that international reform which, as shown in the preceding chapters, in the onward course of civilisation is imperatively needed, the subject naturally divides itself into three branches.

1st, with reference to the *Law*.

2nd, with reference to its *interpretation*.

3rd, with reference to its *enforcement*.

It divides itself naturally into these three branches, because it is an essential difference in these three particulars which constitutes the real distinction between the uncivilised state of society wherein Lynch Law prevails and the more civilised state of society in which it has been supplanted by a civil and judicial system.

Thus Grotius quotes Thucydides to show that a *civil power*—a state—is a body which has its own *laws, tribunals*, and *magistrates*.

A state of society wherein Lynch Law prevails to the full extent is a state of society so unorganised, so uncivilised, as to possess no laws, tribunals, and magistrates—a state of society in which each man's *own* will, whether moral or depraved, is his only recognised law; his *own* judgment, whether sound or biassed, his only recognised judge; his *own* arm, whether weak or powerful, his only weapon of redress.

A civilised state is a society so far organised as to possess established laws, judicial tribunals for their interpretation, and magistrates to enforce them. And the essential distinction between a system of Lynch Law and a civil and judicial system lies therefore in the point, whether the *individual* or the *society* declares, interprets, and enforces the laws whereby social intercourse is regulated.

## CHAPTER II.

*International Law.*

I. THE NECESSITY FOR A MORE COMPLETE SYSTEM OF POSITIVE INTERNATIONAL LAW.

IN an uncivilised state of society wherein Lynch Law prevails to the full extent—*i.e.* wherein no positive civil law exists—men take upon themselves to define what is right and lawful for themselves according to their own notions, instead of obeying a uniform code of laws mutually recognised as equally binding upon all who are members of the same civil society.

It has further been shown that in principle the case is not altered by the fact that, owing to the growth of civilisation, a uniform code of morality is accepted by each as binding upon his own conscience. From the fact that each is bound by his own conscience, it follows as a consequence that no man can be bound by that of any other man. Hence each man, when a common code of morality exists, no less than in its absence, takes upon himself to define what is right and lawful for himself instead of obeying a uniform code of laws mutually recognised as equally binding upon himself and his fellow-subjects.

And this analogy holds good of international society. The fact that, to a large extent, nations have accepted the Grotian international code of morality as binding *in foro conscientiæ* upon civilised nations does not, in itself, change the essential character of international society.

To the extent to which each nation still takes upon itself to define what is right and lawful to itself instead of obeying a uniform code of positive law, mutually recognised by civilised nations as binding upon themselves and their neighbours, to that extent International Lynch Law is the only law in force between nations.

To what extent is this the case?

With a few marked exceptions, such as the Declaration of Paris of 1856 and the declaration that the slave trade shall be piracy, the maxims which now regulate international relations are, in fact, far more analogous to rules of morality binding *in foro conscientiæ* than to the enactment of positive law.

To make the very most of it, they have only *partially* been converted, under the sanction of long international usage, into positive law.

It is true that *some* principles have undoubtedly become established and generally recognised by almost invariable usage, but it is no less true that in other particulars, within certain limits, each nation holds its own views according to its own supposed interests, and a different view from its neighbours when their interests are supposed to be divergent. There is, in many cases, just as much difference of opinion and divergence of policy, as there is apparent contrariety of interest.

Now the position advanced is this: That while the absence of positive law was a tolerable and necessary evil while nations were passing through the self-subsistent stage of national life and had very little mutual intercourse, it is becoming an intolerable and unnecessary evil now that nations are, one after another, passing out of the self-subsistent stage of national life into the most dependent one; and now that the adoption of a free trade policy by one nation after another is more and more blending the interests of all nations in one, entangling the threads of their national prosperity into an international skein.

The position advanced is this: That inevitably, in the present complicated state of international society, the continued prevalence of Lynch Law in this particular does not, and in the future more and more will not and cannot, work; and that the international system requires, in order that it may work, the adoption by civilised nations of a just and uniform system of *positive international law*.

I do not say that necessarily an exhaustive code must be forthwith framed, to be taken at a gulp by all civilised nations—far from it; but I do say that one great and pressing branch of international reform is, beyond all doubt, the gradual and persistent substitution, as time rolls on, of uniform and clearly defined and accepted *positive* international laws on one question after another, for the international maxims of the jurists.

Nor will this position, I confidently trust, be disputed. It has been, I think, sufficiently shown to be strictly in accordance with the spirit and even the express declarations of Grotius and his more recent expounders. I will content myself with adding to their weighty authority the still more weighty authority of the modern solemn declaration of all the civilised powers of the world, without a single exception, to the general principle involved.

The following is the preamble of the ' Declaration of Paris, respecting maritime law, signed by the plenipotentiaries of Great Britain, Austria, France, Prussia, Russia, Sardinia, and Turkey, assembled in Congress at Paris, April 16, 1856 ':

It declares :

> ' That maritime law in time of war has long been the subject of deplorable disputes.
>
> ' That the uncertainty of the law in such a matter gives rise to differences of opinion, which may occasion serious difficulties and even conflicts.
>
> ' That it is consequently advantageous to

establish a uniform doctrine on so important a point.'

The Declaration which follows this preamble (now adopted by forty-six civilised Powers) establishes as between those Powers something like a uniform code of international law regarding the rights of neutrals, and is, therefore, a step precisely in the right direction. The Americans, indeed, refused to concur in this Declaration, but Mr. Seward, in his correspondence in reference to its adoption, paid nevertheless a just tribute to the rightness and pureness of its object.

'The Declaration of Paris is the joint act of forty-six great and enlightened Powers designing to alleviate the evils of maritime war, and promote the first interest of humanity, which is peace.' (*Seward*, September 7, 1861.)

And Earl Russell stated that 'Her Majesty's Government, in concurring in this Declaration, wished to establish a doctrine for all time, with a view to lessen the horrors of war all over the globe. The instructions sent out to Lord Lyons prove' (he said) 'the sincerity of their wish to give permanence and fixity of principles to this part of the Law of Nations.' (*Russell*, August 28, 1861.)

The general principle expressed so forcibly in the above quotations, and applied by the Declaration of Paris to one portion of international law in particular, is precisely the principle urged in this chapter, and it can hardly require further authority or argument to support it.

## II. ARBITRATION NO PROPER SUBSTITUTE OF INTERNATIONAL LAW.

But inasmuch as the proposal to submit international disputes to arbitration has sometimes been represented as a kind of Morison's Pill to cure all international diseases, it may be well to point out clearly that arbitration (however good as a merely temporary and exceptional expedient, failing international law) is contrary to all sound political principles as a permanent substitute for *law*, and as such *it will not work*.

In the first place, it should never be forgotten that the great end of law is not to *decide*, but to *prevent* disputes; that for every dispute which British civil law, *e.g.*, decides there are thousands of cases in which disputes are prevented from arising by its certainty and clearness. But arbitration in itself is powerless to *prevent* disputes; it only extends to the adjustment of disputes which have already arisen.

Arbitration, therefore, as a system fails in fulfilling the main end in view.

2ndly. In another, and scarcely less important particular, arbitration, from its very nature, must fail as a substitute for law. It is under just laws, well defined, and clearly recognised beforehand, and under these alone, that the intricate entanglements of interests can safely exist, without which the advantages of civilised life cannot be realised. In the absence of such laws men's relations to one another are necessarily kept more simple, and men refrain from entering into transactions which otherwise they would enter into daily without the least misgiving, and to mutual advantage.

3rdly. Sublime as the theory of simple justice, dispensed by the untrammeled award of an honest and upright arbiter may be, in practice it would afford no guarantee of individual liberty. It would be open to all the objections which lie against the principle of *legislating for a special case after its occurrence.* It lacks the guarantee of perfect impartiality which constitutes the very essence of laws framed for all cases alike, without any reference either to any particular case which actually occurs, or to the particular parties to a dispute. Consequently, no one in his senses would bind himself beforehand to submit all questions of dispute in which he may become involved to the arbitration even of the best of his friends. It would be to make another man's conscience, and not his own, the guide of his actions.

And so, in international affairs, there are cases where the rights are so plain and the issue so important that it would be folly to hazard the result of an arbitration.

Thus Vattel, whilst strongly recommending a resort to arbitration before an appeal to the sword in doubtful cases which do not involve essential points, expressly distinguishes from them cases of dispute in which the '*essential rights*' or the '*safety of the nation*' is involved (*Vattel*, 278–9), and he brings forward the instance of the Swiss, who have had the precaution in their alliances to 'agree beforehand on the manner in which their disputes were to be submitted to arbitration'—a 'wise precaution which has not a little contributed to maintain the Helvetic Republic in that flourishing state which secures her liberty and renders her respectable throughout Europe.' '*And yet the Swiss*,' he continues, '*on occasions when their liberty was menaced refused to submit their dispute to arbitration.*' (*Vattel*, 278–80.)

Nor is it, moreover, in the least degree likely that nations will bind themselves to submit their disputes to arbitration.

The Plenipotentiaries of the great nations of Europe, assembled in Congress at Paris, though they had unanimously and without scruple agreed to bind themselves, without appeal, by four clearly defined and inexorable laws regarding the rights of maritime powers in time of war; with equal unanimity guarded their *recommendation* that States between which misunderstandings should arise, should, before appealing to arms, have recourse *to the good offices of a friendly power*, with the declaration that it should not amount to an engagement to do so.

The Earl of Clarendon proposed the resolution, as ' calculated to afford to the maintenance of peace a chance of duration hereafter, *without prejudice, however, to the independence of Governments.*' Count Walewski supported the resolution, conceiving it ' to be fully in accordance with the tendencies of our epoch,' while it ' would *not in any way fetter the free action of Governments.*'

Count Buol did not hesitate to concur in it, ' though he could not make in the name of his Court an absolute engagement calculated to limit the independence of the Austrian Cabinet.'

And the Plenipotentiaries did not hesitate to give it the '*most extended application*,' because ' it could not in any case oppose limits to the liberty of judgment, of which no power can divest itself in questions affecting its dignity.'

Such was the jealousy of the great powers of anything approaching to an engagement to resort to even so harmless a course as the *mediation of a friendly power* (for there was nothing said about *arbitration* at this Congress) before resorting to force.

What, then, would be the jealousy with which any scheme would be met for referring international disputes to arbitration?

We may well conclude from the result of the Congress of Paris of 1856 that the whole range of international law may probably be reformed and fixed, by similar declarations to that upon maritime law, before nations are prepared to bind themselves to refer their disputes to arbitration.

Hence we conceive that it cannot be too clearly kept in view, that good as arbitration may be, and doubtless is, in its proper sphere, as an exceptional resort failing international law, to rest upon it as a permanent substitute for law would be to build upon the sand.

It is not needful here to dwell on the subject of 'arbitration' in its own proper sphere, and to urge its more frequent adoption in cases for the settlement of which it is adapted. All that it is needful to point out at this stage of the subject is, that arbitration cannot rightly be held out as a permanent substitute for a system of positive and well-defined law.

### III. THE LIMITS OF INTERNATIONAL LAW—NON-INTERVENTION.

Although a sound system of positive international law may be regarded as essential to the common weal of nations, and as admitting of no such substitute as arbitration, in the present complex state of international society, it is, on the other hand, important to mark clearly the limits within which the range of positive law must itself be confined, and beyond which nations must be left to act according to their own judgment, without legal or other interference.

The range of international law, as well as of individual interference in the affairs of nations, is strictly limited by the doctrine of *non-intervention*.

There is, perhaps, no more encouraging fact in modern international history than the steady advance which has of late been made by nearly all political parties towards the adoption of this doctrine.

There is, indeed, a false doctrine of non-intervention, based upon a selfish policy, which would stand by and see a weaker power oppressed by a stronger one without interference, because it is not the direct interest of the latter at the moment to interfere.

Without saying that a great power like England ought to consider it its business to turn knight-errant and undertake every job of police which *wants* doing on the seas, a selfish policy may safely be denounced as contrary to the laws of natural justice and international morality, which proclaim the equal rights of all nations, be they weak or strong.

The true doctrine of non-intervention rests, not upon the want of direct interest on the part of other nations, but upon the right of international liberty on the part of the nation interfered with.

I

It rests upon the fact that no nation or compact of nations has by nature a *right* to interfere with the private affairs of any *other*, unless such interference be strictly needful to secure the common weal of nations. It is analogous to the law of civil liberty which denies that any individual or state has a right to meddle with the personal rights of the subject, except so far as is needful to secure the common weal. Were *this* doctrine of non-intervention clearly defined and thoroughly accepted by civilised nations, the province of international *law* would be wonderfully narrowed and brought into manageable compass.

But, if this be the true doctrine of non-intervention, it is obvious that the same rules cannot be laid down as the limit of right intervention on the part of individual nations on the one hand, and of international society by its laws on the other.

A distinction must clearly be recognised in international affairs analogous to that which exists between the limits of right intervention in the private affairs of individuals, on the part of individuals, on the one hand, and of the State on the other hand.

An individual has no right to trespass on his neighbour's property, but the State has a right to make roads and railroads over everyone's property whenever the common weal really requires it.

And so an organised international society, if it existed, might probably rightly intervene by its laws in some cases, when it would be injurious and wrong for an isolated nation to do so.

And as the right of intervention is extended by the organisation of a civil or international society, so also are the corresponding obligations.

It is not always the duty of an individual to redress a wrong done even to himself. But it is the duty of a civil society impartially to carry out its laws. And so also of nations and international society.

A nation is not bound to act the knight-errant, or even to enforce all its rightful claims against all other nations. But international positive law once clearly established as an international institution, it will become no less the duty of international than of civil society impartially and promptly to maintain and carry out those laws, as far as the common weal of nations may require it.

Hence the great importance of keeping all attempts at international legislation clearly within the just limits of the true doctrine of non-intervention, so that they may thoroughly enlist the moral support of the international community.

For a law once enacted, which shall infringe unduly the lawful liberty of any nation, must shake the foundations of the whole international fabric. It must entail one of two alternative evils, and probably both. To carry it out would be to perpetrate a legal tyranny. To neglect to put it in force would be to let down the dignity of the law.

To attempt to carry it out, and to fail in the attempt, would be to be gored by both horns of the dilemma, and thus it would submit the international system to a double shock.

And yet no one has been able to draw with logical exactness the practical limits to right intervention on the part of society through its laws, simple as is the theory of non-intervention expressed in general terms. Probably the question no more admits of an universal solution in international than in civil affairs. At all events, it will not be expected that such a solution should be given in this Essay.

I shall content myself, therefore, with having urged the expediency of erring, if at all, on the side of non-intervention, rather than running the risk of shaking the whole international fabric by attempts at unwise intervention.

IV. THE ACTUAL CONSENT OF NATIONS REQUIRED TO MAKE INTERNATIONAL LAW BINDING. A MAJORITY OF NATIONS CANNOT ENACT LAWS WHICH SHALL BE UNIVERSALLY BINDING.

While it may be impossible to give an universal solution to the question where in practice to draw the line of non-intervention, it is not only possible, but absolutely necessary to put *practical guards* upon unjust or undue intervention on the part of society in the affairs of individuals.

The only guard, which in practice has proved itself at all a successful one, is that of obtaining, as nearly as the circumstances of the case will admit, the consent of individuals to the laws which they are bound to obey.

But the right of individuals not to be bound by laws to which they have not given their individual consent, is one of those rights which men have in practice always been compelled partially to give up in civil society.

They do so on the sound principle that all human association, by law of nature, involves that each individual so associating shall give up so much of his individual liberty as is needful to secure the common end, to attain which the society is formed.

The art of civil association consists in obtaining the maximum of common good at the minimum expense of individual rights, so that there may be no *waste* of the latter.

In the case of a nation composed of several millions of people, each individual cannot possibly give his own actual consent to every one of the laws. And hence the exigencies of a civilised nation require the establishment of a sovereign power, capable of making and of enforcing its laws upon all its subjects. And the nearest equivalent to the actual concurrence of all in the acts of the sovereign power which political skill has been able as yet to contrive, is that system of representation and delegation of rights and duties to a comparatively very small number of men, which is as yet far from perfect either in its theory or practice.

Under the civil institutions of the purest republic, as well as of a constitutional monarchy, individual men necessarily so far give up their individual rights to the majority of their fellow-citizens that they become in fact, as well as in name, *subjects* obeying a superior power or government, which can and does constantly make laws affecting their rights without their individual consent to them having been directly obtained or even asked for.

In civil society, therefore, even under the best representative system,—

1. The actual consent of each is not obtained to the laws.
2. The majority impose laws upon themselves and the minority also.

Now, let it be observed how far the analogy between international and civil affairs holds in this respect, and where it breaks down.

By law of nature nations equally with men are so constituted that they cannot associate together for a common good without curtailing to some extent their own individual liberty, and the art of international as of civil association consists therefore in obtaining the maximum of common good at the minimum expense of individual liberty.

But the extent to which it is needful to infringe individual liberty to attain the common good, must obviously differ greatly under differing circumstances. And it would indeed be jumping to a wild conclusion were it assumed that the circumstances of civil and international society are the same. They differ in the most material point.

There are, perhaps, not fifty civilised states in the world, and practically not nearly so many civilised *nations*, for small states for international purposes either are confederated into one nation or follow the leadership of others.

When the most civilised of these states associate together to establish such common positive laws as their common weal requires, it is obvious that the same necessity does not exist, as in the case of a state composed of millions of subjects, either for that system of representation and delegation so essential in the latter, or for the existence of a concentrated sovereign power without which no state could exist.

Even in a populous state, each individual is in theory supposed to have given his consent to the laws through the machinery of representation and delegation alluded to. Much more, therefore, in the case of a few highly civilised nations, so far as the necessity for such machinery does not exist— so far as the circumstances of international society admit of the actual consent of each nation being given to its laws—so far the right of the society to dispense with the *actual consent* of each nation must be absent also.

And also as to the other point intimately connected with the question of individual consent to laws—the right of a majority to bind a minority—how far does it exist in international affairs?

The right of a majority in a state to bind a minority, and the consequent curtailment of the liberties of the minority, rests chiefly upon the modern *territorial* sovereignty of nations, and the consequent necessity of the law having universal jurisdiction over all the inhabitants within a certain geographical area.

This element is wholly absent in international society. Under present circumstances such a society would not rest upon a territorial basis at all —it would embrace, probably, the most civilised nations of the globe, without regard to their geographical position. And therefore there is no difficulty, or at least not the same difficulty, in leaving out dissentient nations, whether a minority or a majority, from the international society. There is no necessity, or at least not the same necessity, for curtailing the rights of dissentient nations so far as to bind them with positive laws enacted by a majority of nations against their will.

Hence we arrive at the conclusion that *positive international law* is binding *as such* only on those nations whose actual assent has been given to its terms. As regards nations who have not given their actual consent to any *positive law*, it has no authority *as such* whatever.

In support of a conclusion so essential to the right understanding of the subject hereafter to be dwelt upon, it may be well to adduce some authority and precedent.

The first illustration to which I shall refer is the prohibition of the slave trade.

Piracy has for long, by universal usage among civilised nations, been considered as contrary to international law. But, until modern times, the slave trade was not looked upon as piracy.

Perhaps there never was a case in which so nearly *universal* a change of feeling among nations has taken place as with reference to the slave trade. If the concerted action of all the greater powers and most of the lesser ones of Europe and America could establish a *positive international law* so as to make it binding upon all nations, including the very small minority who had not given their consent to it, the declaration of the slave trade to be piracy surely must have been the one.

But what is the fact? Although by *positive international law* the slave trade has been declared to be piracy as between all nations who have, by treaty or their own laws, actually assented thereto, yet it is still clearly recognised that it is not *jure gentium* piracy as regards nations who have not thus given their assent.*

* This was clearly stated by Lord Stowell in the case of the

The only other case to which I shall allude in its further confirmation is that of the Treaty of Paris of 1856.

The forty-six civilised nations which alone are bound by the laws of maritime warfare contained in that Declaration all gave their individual and actual consent to its terms.

Their associating for this purpose gave them no sovereign authority over the rest of the world. As between themselves they are bound, to the extent of its terms, by a mutually recognised and uniform law; but nations not parties to the

---

*Louis.* 'The slave trade had been carried on by all nations, including Great Britain, until a very recent period, and was still carried on by Spain and Portugal, and not yet absolutely prohibited by France. It was not, therefore, a criminal traffic by the consuetudinary law of nations, and every nation, *independently of special compact*, retained a legal right to carry it on. No one nation had a right to force the way to the liberation of Africa by trampling on the independence of other States.' (*Wheaton*, 168.)

The Supreme Court of the United States adopted the same conclusion :—

'No principle of general law was more universally acknowledged than the perfect equality of nations. Russia and Geneva have equal rights. It results from this equality, that no one can rightfully impose a rule on another. . . . A right, then, which was vested in all by the consent of all could be divested only by consent. . . . As no nation could prescribe a rule for others, no one could make a law of nations; and this traffic remained [legally] lawful to those whose governments had not forbidden it.'

In 1845 the same principle was again adhered to and confirmed in the case of the *Felicidade* by the majority of the judges, whose decision Dr. Phillimore cites as showing that, notwithstanding the numerous treaties and conventions of civilised nations on the subject, 'the English law does not yet hold slave-trading to be "*jure gentium*" PIRACY.'—*Phil. Int. Law*, i. 333-4.

Declaration are in no way affected by it—they are acknowledged by the Declaration itself as bound only by such rules of international morality as were prevalent before its adoption.

The care with which these points were guarded, both in the preliminary discussion and in the final Declaration, will be sufficiently apparent to any one who may take the trouble to read the protocols of the conferences.

### V. OBJECTIONS ANSWERED.

But, it may be asked, Does not the absence of a sovereign power to enact international laws, and the impossibility of their having a universal jurisdiction within a given geographical area, prevent the existence of any *positive* international laws at all ? Are the rules agreed upon by the few consenting nations, such as those relating to the slave trade and maritime rights, to be regarded as really *positive international laws* ?

The answer is obvious.

Were our only idea of law confined to that with which we are familiar in a modern state, it might possibly be doubtful. And by assuming a definition of positive *Law* to fit this peculiar and restricted idea, no doubt international law may technically be excluded from the range of 'positive law' so defined.

But we are pursuing a *practical* and not merely a

technical argument, and we have therefore to deal not with names but with things.

As before hinted, the idea of territorial sovereignty, as regards civil law, is of comparatively modern birth. Positive Law existed before its adoption, and therefore it cannot be an essential of positive law that it should have exclusive sovereignty within certain geographical limits.

And in like manner the fact of civil law being a rule prescribed by a *sovereign* to a *subject* power is clearly only an accident arising out of the multitude of subjects over which ordinary civil law has force. It has nothing to do with the real essence of *positive law* that it should count its adherents by millions. *Law*, in its essence, may prevail as fully over *six* nations as over *sixty* millions of men; and the question of by what machinery it is enacted, whether by a system of representation and delegation, or by actual consent on the part of all who are bound by it, can have nothing to do with the question whether it is *positive law* or not.

I apprehend that *positive law*, established by unanimous and actual consent of all over whom it has force, is *positive law in its simplest and purest form*, and the most *positive* law which can exist, by whatever name it may technically be distinguished from the more complex forms which law has assumed, as applied, under the idea of modern territorial sovereignty, to the internal regulations of sovereign states.

## CHAPTER III.

*The Interpretation of International Law.*

I. THE INTERPRETATION MUST BE JUDICIAL.

WE now enter upon the second branch of the enquiry, and proceed to examine what international reform is needful with reference to the *interpretation* of international law.

It will readily be admitted that the adoption of positive international laws by all civilised nations would by no means in itself suffice to put an end to the evils involved in the prevalence, to however small an extent, of international Lynch Law. Doubtless the existence of clear and simple positive laws mutually binding upon nations would (as it does between individuals) do more than anything else could do to prevent disputes. The clearer and simpler the law, the rarer must be the disputes. But yet disputes will arise, however simple and clear it may be; and how are such disputes to be settled?

In case of any dispute as to what is the law, how is the law to be interpreted?

The answer to this question involves the examination of the second great point in which civil law differs from Lynch Law. In the one case each individual is left to put his own interpretation even upon such rules and principles of mutual action as may chance to be generally recognised. In the other, the interpretation of the law is not left to the parties in dispute, but a *judicial* and authoritative decision of what is the law is provided, which is binding not only upon the parties in dispute and in the particular quarrel, but upon the *whole community* and *in all* like cases.

At present each nation is left to put its own interpretation even upon such portions of the laws of nations as have already been defined and adopted as binding international law.

Should any of the nations parties to the Declaration of Paris differ in their interpretation of any one of its provisions, no international judicial arrangement exists whereby a decision of what is the law can be obtained which shall be binding upon all the nations parties to the Declaration.

Each nation consults its own law-officers and forms its own opinion as to what is the true interpretation of the law, and acts accordingly. In other words, it 'takes the interpretation of the law into its own hands'—it 'does itself justice.' Consequently in this, as in other particulars, the usages of what in its essence is international Lynch Law still survive between nations.

It is submitted, therefore, that the second great branch of international reform must be the establishment, not necessarily of any fixed judicial tribunal, but of some kind of really *judicial* international machinery for interpreting international law, for giving such an impartial and authoritative decision of what is the law as it should be no stain upon a nation's honour either to sue for or obey.

### II. ARBITRATION NO PROPER SUBSTITUTE FOR THE JUDICIAL INTERPRETATION OF INTERNATIONAL LAW.

Here, again, we cannot but regret that the public mind has been partially drawn off from the true scent by the prominence which has been given in some quarters to the scheme of arbitration. What is really required is, not the decision of an *umpire* but the decision of a *judge* — not the decision of arbitrators, one chosen by each of the disputants, with a special view to the particular dispute, and therefore liable to some extent to the suspicion of being more or less partial, but a decision, given under the authority of the whole society of nations, deciding *what is law* without reference to who may be the disputants;—a decision which shall be binding upon other nations in like cases as well as upon the disputants, and which must, to a large extent, be placed by that very fact beyond suspicion of favouring either party. What is required is, as has been already pointed out, an authoritative judgment which shall settle the disputed point of law for all time, and for all nations over whom the law has force; not merely a clumsy expedient whereby the single dispute in hand may be adjusted. What is required is therefore not a court of arbitration, but something tantamount in principle to an *international judicial tribunal*.

I am glad to be able to quote upon this point the recently-published opinion of Mr. J. S. Mill in his 'Considerations on Representative Government.' Speaking of the United States, he writes: ' The tribunals which act as umpires between the Federal and State Governments naturally also decide all disputes between two States. . . . The usual remedies between nations, war and diplomacy, being precluded by the Federal Union, it is necessary that a *judicial remedy* should supply their place. The Supreme Court of the Federation dispenses international law, and is the first great example of *what is now one of the most prominent wants of civilised society, a real International Tribunal.*' (*Representative Government*, by J. S. Mill, 1861, pp. 305, 6.)

I have already quoted the authority of Wheaton on this subject, and referred the reader to a passage in his work on International Law—a work which has deservedly been regarded as of great authority in international affairs—declaring his opinion that it is an 'imperfect' state of international society 'which acknowledges no permanent authorised judicial expositor of its principles and rules.' (*Wheaton*, p. 57.)

I might refer the reader also to a note of Mr. Chitty, in his English edition of Vattel, for the expression of similar views.

And I think I am not mistaken when I say, that the tide of intelligent feeling in this country has recently turned in favour of the view that a judicial system for the interpretation of international law affords the only sound expositor of it in the settlement of international disputes, and as such *sooner or later* will *ultimately* be adopted by civilised nations.

It seems to me, also, that while the current of feeling is stronger than ever in favour of any peaceable settlement of a dispute rather than *war*, and consequently often in favour of arbitration, as the best ready alternative in cases of urgent present necessity, it cannot be said that any scheme of general arbitration as a permanent substitute for a *judicial* system is any more in favour than it was.

A plank may be a godsend to the shipwrecked mariner, but he would not therefore trust himself to a plank as a permanent means of navigation.

III. THE FORMS OF JUDICIAL INTERPRETATION DISTINGUISHED FROM ITS ESSENCE.

That judicial machinery for interpreting international law will, if the growth of civilisation be not unduly checked, ultimately be provided, there can be no manner of doubt, but that at first, or even eventually, all the forms of a civil tribunal will be found applicable to international affairs, is quite another thing; and it is therefore important clearly to distinguish, as we tried to do with respect to the Law itself, between the *form* and the *essence* of a JUDICIAL mode of interpretation.

The essence of a *judicial* decision consists, as already hinted, in its being issued under the joint authority of the whole community over whom the law has force, and therefore being binding upon all upon whom the law is binding, whether they be parties to the particular dispute or not.

In the case of an ordinary judicial tribunal in a State, the power to give a universally binding decision is delegated to a judge, and in him is concentrated, as it were, the judicial authority of the State.

Individuals have no *direct* voice either in the appointment of the judge or in the judicial decision. They delegate to the Government the power to appoint a judge, and the Government delegates to the judge the power to interpret the law. Thus it is by a double delegation that a judicial decision is obtained which is universally binding upon the community.

But the end attained through the form of this double delegation is in its *essence* what would be attained if all could individually have given their consent to the judicial decision, and have bound themselves to abide by its terms.

Whether, and to what extent, there is the room or the need amongst the comparatively few civilised nations for the early adoption of that system of delegation of rights and duties which becomes an absolute necessity when a nation, composed of millions of citizens, has to act as one organised civil society ; or whether, and to what extent at first, nations may be able to attain the required end by united and concerted action, it is not needful here to determine ; for questions like these have mostly to wait for that gradual practical solution which so often converts the seemingly impossible into the *fait accompli*.

Nevertheless, in the meantime, it may be well earnestly to point to the fact that we *have seen* of late, in the concerted and united action of nations, an approach in an isolated instance to the result we wish to see universally attained.

In the recent affair of the *Trent*, we have seen symptoms of an approach towards the practical attainment of a judicial decision of an international dispute. The opinion of all the Great

Powers of Europe, however informally yet so promptly given, in a tone so earnest that it proved how all nations felt alike concerned in the maintenance of international law, was an approach in many respects to something like the verdict of a jury or the solemn judicial decision of judges, delivered one by one from the bench of a great international Court of Appeal. And the prompt submission to this unanimous judgment of civilised nations, on the part of America, more resembled a dignified obedience to a recognised judicial authority than a giving up of the point in dispute to an armed opponent.

I may be allowed, perhaps, also to point out another approach towards the attainment of a judicial mode of interpretation.

I allude to the reference of questions arising under special treaties to what are called '*mixed* courts,' *i.e.* courts composed of judges appointed by both parties to a treaty instead of only by one. The mixed courts established under the recent treaty with the United States relating to the slave trade may be taken as an instance. This is *one* step at least out of the usages of Lynch Law towards a judicial system. The nations jointly undertake the interpretation of the law agreed upon between them, instead of each taking it into its own hands and doing itself or its own subjects justice.

## IV. JUDICIAL INTERPRETATION LIMITED TO EXISTING POSITIVE LAW.

The question may perhaps be asked, with reference to the present American war, How could a judicial tribunal, if such had existed, have decided the dispute between the Federal and Confederate States?

The answer is that a judicial tribunal, having no legislative power, cannot possibly do more than interpret already existing and *recognised law*. If, as at the present moment, there be no recognised international law deciding the rights involved in a great rebellion or revolution like this, a judicial tribunal, if such had existed, would have had no jurisdiction in the case whatever. But the fact that cases may occur over which, even though a judicial tribunal should exist, it would have no jurisdiction, does not arise from any defect in the judicial theory itself. The defect lies in the absence of positive international laws universally recognised: the very defect which we have already pointed out as a relic of Lynch Law.

But while some uniform principles of international law are already formally recognised by forty-six at least of the civilised powers—we allude of course to the Declaration of Paris regarding the rights of neutrals—there exists as yet no organised judicial machinery for interpreting the laws so recognised. And what is here urged is, that this is a defect in the international system which ought to be supplied.

The moment there is as much as a fragment of established law requiring interpretation, the possibility and the need of a judicial interpretation arises. Were the forty-six nations, parties to the Declaration of Paris, to provide by treaty a judicial mode of interpreting its terms, there would then be the germ of a judicial system, co-extensive with the germ of a uniform code of law; and the jurisdiction of the one would then naturally expand with the area covered by the other.

When forty-six civilised powers again met to make further declarations of what, as between themselves, should be considered as binding international law in other particulars, they would naturally refer the interpretation of the new claims to the same judicial decision; and thus little by little, as one point after another of international law was established by mutual treaty, so little by little would the judicial system also cover a larger and larger area. The number of cases of dispute arising beyond jurisdiction would grow gradually more and more rare, until at length, in the course of civilisation, the international legal and judicial system would as fairly and completely meet and amicably settle the bulk of international disputes, as do already Civil Law and Civil Courts of Justice the private disputes of citizens.

## CHAPTER IV.

*The Enforcement of International Law.*

I. THE ULTIMATE SANCTION OF INTERNATIONAL LAW IS PHYSICAL FORCE.

A SYSTEM of civil law is imperfect, and must fall to the ground, unless it be supported by adequate sanctions; unless it be backed by a sufficient power to secure obedience to it.

It is a great mistake to suppose that the establishment of civil law puts an end to the *régime* of physical force.

The ultimate appeal of civil laws, as also of Lynch Law, is to physical force. The change from Lynch Law to civil law is a change in the possession of the sword; from being worn by the angry disputants, it becomes worn by the law.

In a state of Lynch Law each individual wears his own sword and thereby settles his own dispute, whether in the right or in the wrong. By the establishment of civil law, each individual is bound to keep the peace; he resigns to the State the right and the duty of enforcing the law. Instead of attempting to enforce it himself, he calls upon the concentrated power of the State to enforce it in his behalf.

Now a very little consideration will show that in the present practice of nations, so far as it relates to this particular also, Lynch Law prevails.

The breach of international law, in by far the majority of instances, is at this moment a *casus belli* to the injured nation only. It is left to the injured nation to enforce the law, or allow the breach of it to pass unpunished. The injured nation has no recognised right to call upon any other to aid it in enforcing the law. In fact, precisely as under Lynch Law each individual wears his own sword and settles thereby his own dispute, whether in the right or in the wrong, so at this moment each nation maintains its own army, and therewith settles its own disputes, whether in the right or in the wrong.

How is it possible to deny that the interests of civilisation forbid the continuance of Lynch Law in this respect just as fully and clearly as they forbid its continuance between individuals? Lynch Law leads to the same results between nations as between individuals. It means might instead of right in the one case just as much as in the other. In both cases it clearly does not work for the sword to remain in the hands of the disputants. If at all defensible, such a state of things is defensible only as a temporary expedient until something like judicial machinery be established. When a system of judicial law has been established in the place of Lynch Law, the interests of advancing civilisation, in the name alike of the laws of nature and of Christianity, will surely demand that the sword should be under the direction and control, not of the disputing powers, but of the *law* which is to settle their dispute.

The onus of enforcing the law should rest, *not* upon the injured nation only, but upon *the community of nations*.

## II. HOW INTERNATIONAL FORCE OUGHT TO BE APPLIED.

If physical force be the ultimate sanction of international law, how is that sanction to be applied?

Again we are met by the obvious suggestion that it does not at all follow that because, in a state composed of millions of citizens, a system of delegation and concentration of power into a police force is an absolute necessity, the same system of delegation and concentration is needful to attain a similar end in the case of a score or two of civilised nations.

There may not in the latter case be either the room or the need for it.

The essence of a *civil power* may more readily be attained by united and concerted action between nations. The essence of the thing lies in its being the recognised duty of all the nations *severally* to submit to the law, and in its being the recognised duty of all the nations *jointly* to enforce it upon any delinquent.

If forty-six civilised powers are to unite, *as they have done and we hope they may do* again and again, and bind themselves to observe a uniform code of law, and if they go further, as eventually we trust they may do, and bind themselves mutually to adhere to a judicial interpretation of that law in case of any dispute as to its terms, can they, after that, allow a nation party to such a solemn and binding arrangement to break that law and refuse to obey that judicial decision with impunity? Can they any longer leave the enforcement of such a treaty upon, it may be, a stronger power, to the weaker power who may happen to be the one directly injured by the crime?

Are not at this moment all the nations parties to the Declaration of Paris injured by the breach of it by any one of them? Have not all of them the right to combine to enforce that law which any delinquent nation has bound itself by solemn treaty with them strictly to observe? Is not, in fact, the breach of that Declaration by any nation a *casus belli* to all the forty-five other nations as a community, in spite of assertions in some quarters to the contrary?

And if it be so, and if the number of such Declarations comes in the future to be multiplied, will not nations be compelled, for very convenience, to organise some plan of enforcing their provisions less injurious to themselves and their commerce, and less wasteful of human life, than present modes of warfare?

While, however, the creation, whether by combination or delegation, of an *international force* for the enforcement of international law may seem as needful as that of a *civil power* for the enforcement of civil law, yet it must in fairness be admitted that all the evils of war would not be averted at once by its creation. The management of an international police force, however constituted, would doubtless be liable to precisely the same dangers and difficulties to which a civil police force is liable in times of riot and rebellion. Human blood would occasionally still be shed and human passions roused, and the international system would be liable to revolutions and temporary subversion, such as civil powers have had again and again to contend with. There is no royal road to perfection in international any more than in civil affairs. Yet still at the same time, fully admitting the difficulties, there are three points in which the analogy of the history of civil law appears to warrant the belief that they would not in the long run prove insurmountable.

The first point is, that as in the case of civil law the concentration of the physical force in the hands of the civil power has in most nations gradually led to the general disarmament of individuals, so, in the case of international law, the knowledge on the part of nations that the law would be backed by the combined forces of all nations against any delinquent, would lead to a gradually increasing reliance on the protection of international law, and a gradually decreasing reliance merely on their own military establishments.

These latter would gradually become less and less needed, and, ceasing to be a necessity, they would soon cease to be maintained on their present gigantic scale; a mutual reduction in armaments would become obvious and natural, and at the same time reasonable; and possibly in the course of time mutual disarmament might even result.

The second point is, that as in the history of civil law it has been found in practice to be the case, so in the history of international law there is every reason to expect that as civilisation advances the number of cases in which nations would refuse to obey a judicial decision, to obey which they had bound themselves by solemn treaty, and in which the last resort of physical force really would have to be resorted to, would become more and more rare.

The third point is, that in the few cases which might arise in which resort was necessary to physical force to enforce international law, it would come to be applied, as to a large extent it has come to be applied in the case of civil law, more and more wisely and justly as civilisation advances, until ultimately it might be applied, when needful, in a way which would be felt to involve no waste of human blood or human rights.

## CHAPTER V.

### SUMMARY OF THE FOREGOING ARGUMENT.

It now remains to sum up the practical conclusions arrived at in the foregoing pages.

1. The interdependence of nations, and their association in international society, was shown to be the result, not merely of human contrivance, but of certain laws of nature.

2. The answer to the question, how far any nation can remain in a self-subsistent state, or how far it must become dependent upon international intercourse, was shown to rest, not merely upon the intention of its rulers, but mainly upon its own economic condition, inherited from its past history.

3. The economic history and condition of the nations most dependent upon international commerce was carefully reviewed, and the conclusion arrived at that their dependence on foreign trade was likely, not only to continue, but also to increase.

4. The tendency of those nations not yet belonging to the most dependent class was shown to be inevitably *towards* a greater and greater dependence on international trade.

5. The case of young nations, and partially civilised nations, was also alluded to, and it was

remarked that, although international intercourse be not so much a necessity to them as to older nations, it is necessary to the enjoyment of their peculiar wealth; while the dependence of the older nations upon them is increasing every year.

6. The result of this gradually increasing interdependence of civilised nations was shown to be twofold:

> 1st. Modern modes of warfare are becoming more and more injurious to neutrals.
>
> 2nd. They are at the same time becoming less and less effective in the hands of belligerents.

7. The reform of these modes of warfare, so as to make them less injurious to neutrals, was shown to be inevitable. But at the same time their reform was shown to involve their becoming even still less effective than they are.

8. Hence the conclusion was arrived at, that a more radical reform was needful than that of the mere modes of warfare.

9. The radical defect in the international system was traced to the subsistence of what is, in fact, the *régime* of international *Lynch Law* in a state of international society, to meet the needs of which it is wholly inadequate.

10. In accordance with the authority of the great international jurists, the only radical cure for this radical defect was shown to be the substitution of a system of *positive* international law.

11. Any system of positive law was shown to involve three points—
    1. Its enactment.
    2. Its interpretation.
    3. Its enforcement.

And it was shown that the essential distinction between positive law and Lynch Law consisted in the enactment, interpretation, and enforcement of the law being the joint act of the community of nations, rather than being left for each individual nation to do it for itself.

12. The enactment of positive international laws was shown to require the actual consent of all nations to be bound by them. And the Declaration of Paris was alluded to as in its preamble asserting the necessity for positive international laws, and as in itself a practical precedent of the mode of enacting them.

13. It was shown, with reference to the interpretation of international law, that it must be *judicial*—*i.e.* that it must be given under the joint authority of all parties to the law. From this it was shown to result that such judicial interpretation must be strictly confined to what may have been already constituted positive international law; while that, with reference to such *positive law* already enacted, as *e.g.* the Declaration of Paris, the parties to its enactment are even now in reality committed to its joint or judicial interpretation in some way or other, though no machinery

has been yet organised for carrying out the object in practice.

14. With reference to the enforcement of positive international law, it was shown that, after its enactment by the joint act of several nations, it ought to be *jointly* enforced, and that, although no joint method of enforcing it has been organised, if one nation, party to the Declaration of Paris, *e.g.*, were to refuse compliance with its provisions, the remaining parties to it stand committed to its joint enforcement in some way or other.

And now in conclusion, in thus looking at these international problems *as one whole*—tracing back through the links of cause and effect the onward course of civilisation, marking how, under the laws of political economy, one thing has led to another, how the past has led to the present and the present is leading to an inevitable future,—who can fail to be impressed with the *irresistibility* of the current which seems to be bearing us onward? If the laws which are fixed in the constitution of things, and which regulate the civil and political relations of mankind, be as irreversible by man as are the laws of physical science; if human will, whether of kings or parliaments, be as powerless to reverse the laws of political economy as the law of gravitation; and if, under the operation of those laws, the onward course of civilisation has compelled nations, and especially England, to adopt the commercial policy to which they are so fully committed,—if such a policy is really inconsistent with the continuance of Lynch Law between nations, and requires as its corollary the substitution of a legal and judicial system, then, so far from such a result appearing Utopian, it must, in view of the irresistible march of civilisation, eventually certainly come. Its accomplishment can only be a question of time.

What, then, is the practical duty of statesmen? It must be this:—

It behoves the statesmen of civilised nations, and especially of England, in all their attempts to rectify international relations, not only to keep steadily in view the ultimate attainment of a legal and judicial substitute for International Lynch Law, but also by every means in their power to make tentative approaches towards it. They cannot undo the economic history of the past. They cannot reverse the tendency to the increasing interdependence of nations which is the result of their present economic condition. They cannot bend the inexorable laws of nature to make them fit an international system which belongs to the past. Their business is to reform the International system, and to make it meet the needs of advancing international civilisation.

# POSTSCRIPT

ON THE RELATION OF THE REFORM ADVOCATED IN THE FOREGOING ESSAY TO THE LATE MR. COBDEN'S POLICY OF NON-INTERVENTION.

---

It may be well to add a few words to point out the relation which the policy advocated in the foregoing Essay bears to that policy of non-intervention which was advocated with so much force by the late Mr. Cobden.

I believe that, the two policies are not antagonistic, but that each is, in fact, strictly speaking, the complement of the other.

No one urged more strongly than did Mr. Cobden the fact that we are rapidly passing into a stage of civilisation in which the well-being of the *people* of all nations requires that the great economic principle of division and co-operation of labour should be fully applied, not within the limits of each nation only, but also to the whole world. So far as regards the interchange of products and manufactures, he held that there should be no international barriers. This is what he meant by 'free trade.'

Mr. Cobden went further, and laid down the

principle that a policy of free trade, if consistently carried out, involves the freedom of commerce from the risks of war. And he urged that the rights of belligerent nations under international law should be curtailed, so as to secure that commerce should be as far as possible unmolested by their exercise. (Mr. Cobden's Speeches, II. p. 299.)

He urged that the scope of the rules of international law laid down by the Treaty of Paris of 1856 should be so widened as to secure this object.

Nor did Mr. Cobden shrink from the consequence, that any breach of such a law by a nation would necessitate the intervention of the community of nations in its support. On the contrary, he relied upon the fact that a nation breaking the law would be bringing down upon itself the united power of the whole community of nations, as giving so serious a sanction to international law that in practice it would not be likely to be broken :—

> We have this guarantee, that the international rules I am now advocating will be respected : they are not contemplated to be merely an article in a treaty between any two powers, but to be fundamental *laws* regulating the intercourse of nations, and having the assent of the majority of, if not all, the maritime powers in the world. . . The nation which has been a party to a general system of International Law becomes an outlaw to all nations if it breaks its engagement towards any one. . . I don't rely on the honour of the individual nation . . . for observing the law : I rely upon its being her interest to keep it, because if she were at war with us, and were to break the law, she would not

break it as against us alone, but as against the whole world. (*Cobden's Speeches*, II. p. 300.)

The reform advocated in this Essay is, therefore, a reform which, in measure at least, Mr. Cobden himself recognised as necessary, and as in full harmony with his policy of non-intervention.

On the other hand, the policy of non-intervention is the necessary complement of the policy here advocated. As stated in this Essay, the principle of non-intervention rests upon the right of each nation not to be interfered with in its own free action, except so far as is needful to secure the common weal of nations. In so far, therefore, as the common weal of nations is placed, by the adoption of a system of positive International Law, under the protection of the community of nations, a limit is at once put to the right and necessity of individual intervention, and the excuse for it taken away.

To take a practical case :—Had the war between France and Germany arisen out of a direct breach by one of the two nations of some point of international law clearly settled by some such treaty as the Treaty of Paris of 1856, the nations, parties to such treaty, would, according to the principles urged in this essay, have been placed under the direct obligation *jointly* to intervene in some way or other to prevent the breach of International Law. There would be then no such excuse for individual intervention as there might be were the clearly recognised International Law, which was broken, *not* clearly recognised to be under the joint protection of the community of nations.

There was indeed, in the case which has occurred, no solid ground, according to the principles urged in this essay, for the *joint* intervention of other nations. And why? Because there was no clearly defined and recognised International Law existing, the breach of which was the cause of the war.

Much less was there any solid ground for *individual* intervention. Under existing International Law the war between France and Germany was merely a private quarrel between two nations; and, therefore, for England to have interfered by armed intervention, would have been intervention without legal warrant in the private affairs of two nations, and so would have been clearly a breach of the principle of non-intervention laid down in this essay. It would have been, in fact, a rash assumption by England in Europe of the position assumed by Judge Lynch in Virginia, when he took the law into his own hands and set the representative example of Lynch Law.

Such a policy would not have been, in my opinion, a wise policy for England to have pursued. There seems to me to be nobler work for her to do among the nations than this would have been.

Let England throw the weight of her influence

into the work of simplifying and obtaining the consent of the civilised nations to just international *laws*. Let her at the same time pursue strictly the policy of non-intervention in the *affairs* of other nations so earnestly urged by Mr. Cobden. Let her acquire, by firm and consistent adherence to these principles, the confidence of other nations in her absolute international integrity. Let her at the same time set an example of earnest determination to grapple with her own internal evils, to raise the character of her people, and to secure to them the full inheritance of freedom. Thus to set an example of a free nation desiring and respecting the freedom of other nations, will do more to extend the influence of England than any policy of intervention or international knight-errantry could possibly do.

F. S.

1871.

LONDON: PRINTED BY
SPOTTISWOODE AND CO., NEW-STREET SQUARE
AND PARLIAMENT STREET

39 Paternoster Row, E.C.
London: *January* 1871.

# GENERAL LIST OF WORKS

PUBLISHED BY

## Messrs. LONGMANS, GREEN, READER, and DYER.

| | |
|---|---|
| Arts, Manufactures, &c. ............... 12 | Index ...................................... 21—24 |
| Astronomy, Meteorology, Popular Geography, &c. ..................... 7 | Miscellaneous Works and Popular Metaphysics ............................ 6 |
| Biographical Works .................. 3 | Natural History & Popular Science 8 |
| Chemistry, Medicine, Surgery, and the Allied Sciences .................... 9 | Periodical Publications ............... 20 |
| | Poetry and The Drama ................ 18 |
| Commerce, Navigation, and Mercantile Affairs ......................... 19 | Religious and Moral Works ......... 14 |
| | Rural Sports, &c. ......................... 19 |
| Criticism, Philology, &c. ............... 4 | Travels, Voyages, &c. ................ 16 |
| Fine Arts and Illustrated Editions 11 | Works of Fiction ....................... 17 |
| History, Politics, and Historical Memoirs ................................ 1 | Works of Utility and General Information ........................... 20 |

---

## *History, Politics, Historical Memoirs, &c.*

**The History of England from** the fall of Wolsey to the Defeat of the Spanish Armada. By James Anthony Froude, M.A.

Cabinet Edition, 12 vols. cr. 8vo. £3 12s.
Library Edition, 12 vols. 8vo. £8 18s.

**The History of England from** the Accession of James II. By Lord Macaulay.

Library Edition, 5 vols. 8vo. £4.
Cabinet Edition, 8 vols. post 8vo. 48s.
People's Edition, 4 vols. crown 8vo. 16s.

**Lord Macaulay's Works.** Complete and uniform Library Edition. Edited by his Sister, Lady Trevelyan. 8 vols. 8vo. with Portrait, price £5 5s. cloth, or £8 8s. bound in tree-calf by Rivière.

**An Essay on the History of the** English Government and Constitution, from the Reign of Henry VII. to the Present Time. By John Earl Russell. Fourth Edition, revised. Crown 8vo. 6s.

**Selections from Speeches of Earl** Russell, 1817 to 1841, and from Despatches, 1859 to 1865; with Introductions. 2 vols. 8vo. 28s.

**Varieties of Vice-Regal Life.** By Major-General Sir William Denison, K.C.B. late Governor-General of the Australian Colonies, and Governor of Madras. With Two Maps. 2 vols. 8vo. 28s.

**On Parliamentary Government** in England: its Origin, Development, and Practical Operation. By Alpheus Todd, Librarian of the Legislative Assembly of Canada. 2 vols. 8vo. price £1 17s.

**The Constitutional History of** England since the Accession of George III. 1760—1860. By Sir Thomas Erskine May, K.C.B. Second Edit. 2 vols. 8vo. 33s.

**A Historical Account of the Neu-** trality of Great Britain during the American Civil War. By Montague Bernard, M.A. Royal 8vo. price 16s.

**The History of England,** from the Earliest Times to the Year 1866. By C. D. Yonge, Regius Professor of Modern History in the Queen's University, Belfast. New Edition. Crown 8vo. 7s. 6d.

**A History of Wales,** derived from Authentic Sources. By Jane Williams, Ysgafell, Author of a Memoir of the Rev. Thomas Price, and Editor of his Literary Remains. 8vo. 14s.

A

**Lectures on the History of England**, from the Earliest Times to the Death of King Edward II. By WILLIAM LONGMAN. With Maps and Illustrations. 8vo. 15s.

**The History of the Life and Times** of Edward the Third. By WILLIAM LONGMAN. With 9 Maps, 8 Plates, and 16 Woodcuts. 2 vols. 8vo. 28s.

**History of Civilization in England** and France, Spain and Scotland. By HENRY THOMAS BUCKLE. New Edition of the entire work, with a complete INDEX. 3 vols. crown 8vo. 24s.

**Realities of Irish Life.** By W. STEUART TRENCH, Land Agent in Ireland to the Marquess of Lansdowne, the Marquess of Bath, and Lord Digby. Fifth Edition. Crown 8vo. 6s.

**The Student's Manual of the** History of Ireland. By M. F. CUSACK, Authoress of the 'Illustrated History of Ireland, from the Earliest Period to the Year of Catholic Emancipation.' Crown 8vo. price 6s.

**A Student's Manual of the History** of India, from the Earliest Period to the Present. By Colonel MEADOWS TAYLOR, M.R.A.S. M.R.I.A. Crown 8vo. with Maps, 7s. 6d.

**The History of India,** from the Earliest Period to the close of Lord Dalhousie's Administration. By JOHN CLARK MARSHMAN. 3 vols. crown 8vo. 22s. 6d.

**Indian Polity:** a View of the System of Administration in India. By Lieut.-Col. GEORGE CHESNEY. Second Edition, revised, with Map. 8vo. 21s.

**Home Politics:** being a Consideration of the Causes of the Growth of Trade in relation to Labour, Pauperism, and Emigration. By DANIEL GRANT. 8vo. 7s.

**Democracy in America.** By ALEXIS DE TOCQUEVILLE. Translated by HENRY REEVE. 2 vols. 8vo. 21s.

**Waterloo Lectures:** a Study of the Campaign of 1815. By Colonel CHARLES C. CHESNEY, R.E. late Professor of Military Art and History in the Staff College. Second Edition. 8vo. with Map, 10s. 6d.

**The Military Resources of Prussia** and France, and Recent Changes in the Art of War. By Lieut.-Col. CHESNEY, R.E. and HENRY REEVE, D.C.L. Crown 8vo. 7s. 6d.

**The Overthrow of the Germanic** Confederation by Prussia in 1866. By Sir A. MALET, Bart. K.B.C. late H.B.M. Envoy and Minister at Frankfort. With 5 Maps. 8vo. 18s.

**The Oxford Reformers**—John Colet, Erasmus, and Thomas More; being a History of their Fellow-Work. By FREDERIC SEEBOHM. Second Edition. 8vo. 14s.

**History of the Reformation in** Europe in the Time of Calvin. By J. H. MERLE D'AUBIGNÉ, D.D. VOLS. I. and II. 8vo. 28s. VOL. III. 12s. VOL. IV. price 16s. and VOL. V. price 16s.

**Chapters from French History;** St. Louis, Joan of Arc, Henri IV. with Sketches of the Intermediate Periods. By J. H. GURNEY, M.A. New Edition. Fcp. 8vo. 6s. 6d.

**The History of Greece.** By C. THIRLWALL, D.D. Lord Bishop of St. David's. 8 vols. fcp. 28s.

**The Tale of the Great Persian** War, from the Histories of Herodotus. By GEORGE W. COX, M.A. late Scholar of Trin. Coll. Oxon. Fcp. 3s. 6d.

**Greek History from Themistocles** to Alexander, in a Series of Lives from Plutarch. Revised and arranged by A. H. CLOUGH. Fcp. with 44 Woodcuts, 6s.

**Critical History of the Language** and Literature of Ancient Greece. By WILLIAM MURE, of Caldwell. 5 vols. 8vo. £3 9s.

**History of the Literature of** Ancient Greece. By Professor K. O. MÜLLER. Translated by LEWIS and DONALDSON. 3 vols. 8vo. 21s.

**The History of Rome.** By WILHELM IHNE. Translated and revised by the Author. VOLS. I. and II. 8vo. [*Just ready.*

**History of the City of Rome from** its Foundation to the Sixteenth Century of the Christian Era. By THOMAS H. DYER, LL.D. 8vo. with 2 Maps, 15s.

**History of the Romans under** the Empire. By Very Rev. CHARLES MERIVALE, D.C.L. Dean of Ely. 8 vols. post 8vo. price 48s.

**The Fall of the Roman Republic;** a Short History of the Last Century of the Commonwealth. By the same Author. 12mo. 7s. 6d.

**Historical and Chronological Encyclopædia;** comprising Chronological Notices of all the Great Events of Universal History, including Treaties, Alliances, Wars, Battles, &c.; Incidents in the Lives of Eminent Men, Scientific and Geographical Discoveries, Mechanical Inventions, and Social, Domestic, and Economical Improvements. By the late B. B. WOODWARD, B.A. and W. L. R. CATES. 1 vol. 8vo.
[*In the press.*

**History of European Morals from** Augustus to Charlemagne. By W. E. H. LECKY, M.A. 2 vols. 8vo. price 28s.

**History of the Rise and Influence of the Spirit of Rationalism in Europe.** By the same Author. Cabinet Edition (the Fourth). 2 vols. crown 8vo. price 16s.

**God in History;** or, the Progress of Man's Faith in the Moral Order of the World. By the late Baron BUNSEN. Translated from the German by SUSANNA WINKWORTH; with a Preface by Dean STANLEY 3 vols. 8vo. 42s.

**Socrates and the Socratic Schools.** Translated from the German of Dr. E. ZELLER, with the Author's approval, by the Rev. OSWALD J. REICHEL, B.C.L. and M.A. Crown 8vo. 8s. 6d.

**The Stoics, Epicureans, and** Sceptics. Translated from the German of Dr. E. ZELLER, with the Author's approval, by OSWALD J. REICHEL, B.C.L. and M.A. Crown 8vo. 14s.

**The History of Philosophy, from** Thales to Comte. By GEORGE HENRY LEWES. Third Edition, rewritten and enlarged. 2 vols. 8vo. 30s.

**The Mythology of the Aryan Nations.** By GEORGE W. COX, M.A. late Scholar of Trinity College, Oxford. 2 vols. 8vo. price 28s.

**The English Reformation.** By F. C. MASSINGBERD, M.A. Chancellor of Lincoln. 4th Edition, revised. Fcp. 7s. 6d.

**Maunder's Historical Treasury;** comprising a General Introductory Outline of Universal History, and a Series of Separate Histories. Fcp. 6s.

**Critical and Historical Essays** contributed to the *Edinburgh Review* by the Right Hon. Lord MACAULAY:—
CABINET EDITION, 4 vols. 24s.
LIBRARY EDITION, 3 vols. 8vo. 36s.
PEOPLE'S EDITION, 2 vols. crown 8vo. 8s.
STUDENT'S EDITION, crown 8vo. 6s.

**History of the Early Church,** from the First Preaching of the Gospel to the Council of Nicæa, A.D. 325. By the Author of 'Amy Herbert.' New Edition. Fcp. 4s. 6d.

**Sketch of the History of the** Church of England to the Revolution of 1688. By the Right Rev. T. V. SHORT, D.D. Lord Bishop of St. Asaph. Eighth Edition. Crown 8vo. 7s. 6d.

**History of the Christian Church,** from the Ascension of Christ to the Conversion of Constantine. By E. BURTON, D.D late Regius Prof. of Divinity in the University of Oxford. Fcp. 3s. 6d.

*Biographical Works.*

**The Life of Isambard Kingdom** Brunel, Civil Engineer. By ISAMBARD BRUNEL, B.C.L. of Lincoln's Inn, Chancellor of the Diocese of Ely. With Portrait, Plates, and Woodcuts. 8vo. 21s.

**The Life and Letters of the Rev.** Sydney Smith. Edited by his Daughter, Lady HOLLAND, and Mrs. AUSTIN. New Edition, complete in One Volume. Crown 8vo. price 6s.

**A Memoir of G. E. L. Cotton,** D.D. late Lord Bishop of Calcutta; with Selections from his Journals and Letters. Edited by Mrs. COTTON. With Portrait. 8vo.
[*Just ready.*

**Some Memorials of R. D. Hampden,** Bishop of Hereford. Edited by his Daughter, HENRIETTA HAMPDEN. With Portrait. 8vo.
[*Just ready.*

**The Life and Travels of George** Whitefield, M.A. of Pembroke College, Oxford, Chaplain to the Countess of Huntingdon. By J. P. GLEDSTONE. Post 8vo.
[*Just ready.*

**Memoir of Pope Sixtus the Fifth.** By Baron HÜBNER. Translated from the Original in French, with the Author's sanction, by HUBERT E. H. JERNINGHAM. 2 vols. 8vo.
[*In the press.*

**The Life and Letters of Faraday.** By Dr. BENCE JONES, Secretary of the Royal Institution. Second Edition, with Portrait and Woodcuts. 2 vols. 8vo. 28s.

**Faraday as a Discoverer.** By JOHN TYNDALL, LL.D. F.R.S. Professor of Natural Philosophy in the Royal Institution. New and Cheaper Edition, with Two Portraits. Fcp. 8vo. 3s. 6d.

**Lives of the Lord Chancellors** and Keepers of the Great Seal of Ireland, from the Earliest Times to the Reign of Queen Victoria. By J. R. O'FLANAGAN, M.R.I.A. Barrister. 2 vols. 8vo. 36s.

**Dictionary of General Biography;** containing Concise Memoirs and Notices of the most Eminent Persons of all Countries, from the Earliest Ages to the Present Time. Edited by WILLIAM L. R. CATES. 8vo. price 21s.

**Memoirs of Baron Bunsen,** drawn chiefly from Family Papers by his Widow, FRANCES Baroness BUNSEN. Second Edition, abridged; with 2 Portraits and 4 Woodcuts. 2 vols. post 8vo. 21s.

**The Letters of the Right Hon.** Sir George Cornewall Lewis to various Friends. Edited by his Brother, the Rev. Canon Sir G. F. LEWIS, Bart. 8vo. with Portrait, 14s.

**Life of the Duke of Wellington.** By the Rev. G. R. GLEIG, M.A. Popular Edition, carefully revised; with copious Additions. Crown 8vo. with Portrait, 5s.

**Father Mathew: a Biography.** By JOHN FRANCIS MAGUIRE, M.P. Popular Edition, with Portrait. Crown 8vo. 3s. 6d.

**History of my Religious Opinions.** By J. H. NEWMAN, D.D. Being the Substance of Apologia pro Vitâ Suâ. Post 8vo. price 6s.

**Letters and Life of Francis** Bacon, including all his Occasional Works. Collected and edited, with a Commentary, by J. SPEDDING. VOLS. I. & II. 8vo. 24s. VOLS. III. & IV. 24s. VOL. V. 12s.

**Felix Mendelssohn's Letters from** *Italy and Switzerland*, and *Letters* from 1833 to 1847, translated by Lady WALLACE. With Portrait. 2 vols. crown 8vo. 5s. each.

**Memoirs of Sir Henry Havelock,** K.C.B. By JOHN CLARK MARSHMAN. People's Edition, with Portrait. Crown 8vo. price 3s. 6d.

**Essays in Ecclesiastical Biography.** By the Right Hon. Sir J. STEPHEN, LL.D. Cabinet Edition. Crown 8vo. 7s. 6d.

**The Earls of Granard:** a Memoir of the Noble Family of Forbes. Written by Admiral the Hon. JOHN FORBES, and Edited by GEORGE ARTHUR HASTINGS, present Earl of Granard, K.P. 8vo. 10s.

**Vicissitudes of Families.** By Sir J. BERNARD BURKE, C.B. Ulster King of Arms. New Edition, remodelled and enlarged. 2 vols. crown 8vo. 21s.

**Lives of the Tudor Princesses,** including Lady Jane Grey and her Sisters. By AGNES STRICKLAND. Post 8vo. with Portrait, &c. 12s. 6d.

**Lives of the Queens of England.** By AGNES STRICKLAND. Library Edition, newly revised; with Portraits of every Queen, Autographs, and Vignettes. 8 vols. post 8vo. 7s. 6d. each.

**Maunder's Biographical Treasury.** Thirteenth Edition, reconstructed and partly re-written, with above 1,000 additional Memoirs, by W. L. R. CATES. Fcp. 6s.

---

## Criticism, Philosophy, Polity, &c.

**The Subjection of Women.** By JOHN STUART MILL. New Edition. Post 8vo. 5s.

**On Representative Government.** By JOHN STUART MILL. Third Edition. 8vo. 9s. crown 8vo. 2s.

**On Liberty.** By the same Author. Fourth Edition. Post 8vo. 7s. 6d. Crown 8vo. 1s. 4d.

**Principles of Political Economy.** By the same. Sixth Edition. 2 vols. 8vo. 30s. or in 1 vol. crown 8vo. 5s.

**Utilitarianism.** By the same. 3d Edit. 8vo. 5s.

**Dissertations and Discussions.** By the same Author. Second Edition. 3 vols. 8vo. 36s.

**Examination of Sir W. Hamilton's** Philosophy, and of the principal Philosophical Questions discussed in his Writings. By the same. Third Edition. 8vo. 16s.

**Inaugural Address** delivered to the University of St. Andrews. By JOHN STUART MILL. 8vo. 5s. Crown 8vo. 1s.

**Analysis of the Phenomena of the Human Mind.** By JAMES MILL. A New Edition, with Notes, Illustrative and Critical, by ALEXANDER BAIN, ANDREW FINDLATER, and GEORGE GROTE. Edited, with additional Notes, by JOHN STUART MILL. 2 vols. 8vo. price 28s.

**The Elements of Political Economy.** By HENRY DUNNING MACLEOD, M.A. Barrister-at-Law. 8vo. 16s.

**A Dictionary of Political Economy;** Biographical, Bibliographical, Historical, and Practical. By the same Author. VOL. I. royal 8vo. 30s.

**Lord Bacon's Works, collected** and edited by R. L. ELLIS, M.A. J. SPEDDING, M.A. and D. D. HEATH. New and Cheaper Edition. 7 vols. 8vo. price £3 13s. 6d.

**A System of Logic, Ratiocinative** and Inductive. By JOHN STUART MILL. Seventh Edition. 2 vols. 8vo. 25s.

**Analysis of Mr. Mill's System of Logic.** By W. STEBBING, M.A. New Edition. 12mo. 3s. 6d.

**The Institutes of Justinian;** with English Introduction, Translation, and Notes. By T. C. SANDARS, M.A. Barrister-at-Law. New Edition. 8vo. 15s.

**The Ethics of Aristotle;** with Essays and Notes. By Sir A. GRANT, Bart. M.A. LL.D. Second Edition, revised and completed. 2 vols. 8vo. price 28s.

**The Nicomachean Ethics of Aristotle.** Newly translated into English. By R. WILLIAMS, B.A. Fellow and late Lecturer Merton College, Oxford. 8vo. 12s.

**Bacon's Essays, with Annotations.** By R. WHATELY, D.D. late Archbishop of Dublin. Sixth Edition. 8vo. 10s. 6d.

**Elements of Logic.** By R. WHATELY, D.D. late Archbishop of Dublin. New Edition. 8vo. 10s. 6d. crown 8vo. 4s. 6d.

**Elements of Rhetoric.** By the same Author. New Edition. 8vo. 10s. 6d. Crown 8vo. 4s. 6d.

**English Synonymes.** By E. JANE WHATELY. Edited by Archbishop WHATELY. 5th Edition. Fcp. 3s.

**An Outline of the Necessary Laws of Thought:** a Treatise on Pure and Applied Logic. By the Most Rev. W. THOMSON, D.D. Archbishop of York. Ninth Thousand. Crown 8vo. 5s. 6d.

**The Election of Representatives,** Parliamentary and Municipal; a Treatise. By THOMAS HARE, Barrister-at-Law. Third Edition, with Additions. Crown 8vo. 6s.

**Speeches of the Right Hon. Lord MACAULAY,** corrected by Himself. People's Edition, crown 8vo. 3s. 6d.

**Lord Macaulay's Speeches on** Parliamentary Reform in 1831 and 1832. 16mo. price ONE SHILLING.

**Walker's Pronouncing Dictionary** of the English Language. Thoroughly revised Editions, by B. H. SMART. 8vo. 12s. 16mo. 6s.

**A Dictionary of the English Language.** By R. G. LATHAM, M.A. M.D. F.R.S. Founded on the Dictionary of Dr. S. JOHNSON, as edited by the Rev. H. J. TODD, with numerous Emendations and Additions. 4 vols. 4to. price £7.

**Thesaurus of English Words and Phrases,** classified and arranged so as to facilitate the expression of Ideas, and assist in Literary Composition. By P. M. ROGET, M.D. New Edition. Crown 8vo. 10s. 6d.

**The Debater;** a Series of Complete Debates, Outlines of Debates, and Questions for Discussion. By F. ROWTON. Fcp. 6s.

**Lectures on the Science of Language,** delivered at the Royal Institution. By MAX MÜLLER, M.A. &c. Foreign Member of the French Institute. 2 vols. 8vo. price 30s.

**Chapters on Language.** By F. W. FARRAR, M.A. F.R.S. late Fellow of Trin. Coll. Cambridge. Crown 8vo. 8s. 6d.

**A Book about Words.** By G. F. GRAHAM. Fcp. 8vo. 3s. 6d.

**Southey's Doctor,** complete in One Volume, edited by the Rev. J. W. WARTER, B.D. Square crown 8vo. 12s. 6d.

**Historical and Critical Commentary on the Old Testament;** with a New Translation. By M. M. KALISCH, Ph.D. Vol. I. *Genesis,* 8vo. 18s. or adapted for the General Reader, 12s. Vol. II. *Exodus,* 15s. or adapted for the General Reader, 12s. Vol III. *Leviticus,* Part I. 15s. or adapted for the General Reader, 8s.

**A Hebrew Grammar, with Exercises.** By the same. Part I. *Outlines with Exercises,* 8vo. 12s. 6d. KEY, 5s. Part II. *Exceptional Forms and Constructions,* 12s. 6d.

**Manual of English Literature,** Historical and Critical: with a Chapter on English Metres. By THOMAS ARNOLD, M.A. Second Edition. Crown 8vo. 7s. 6d.

**A Latin-English Dictionary.** By J. T. WHITE, D.D. of Corpus Christi College, and J. E. RIDDLE, M.A. of St. Edmund Hall, Oxford. Third Edition, revised. 2 vols. 4to. pp. 2,128, price 42s.

**White's College Latin-English Dictionary** (Intermediate Size), abridged from the Parent Work for the use of University Students. Medium 8vo. pp. 1,048, price 18s.

**White's Junior Student's Complete Latin-English and English-Latin Dictionary.** Revised Edition. Square 12mo. pp. 1,058, price 12s.

Separately { ENGLISH-LATIN, 5s. 6d.
{ LATIN-ENGLISH, 7s. 6d.

**An English-Greek Lexicon,** containing all the Greek Words used by Writers of good authority. By C. D. YONGE, B.A. New Edition. 4to. 21s.

**Mr. Yonge's New Lexicon,** English and Greek, abridged from his larger work (as above). Square 12mo. 8s. 6d.

**The Mastery of Languages;** or, the Art of Speaking Foreign Tongues Idiomatically. By THOMAS PRENDERGAST, late of the Civil Service at Madras. Second Edition. 8vo. 6s.

**A Greek-English Lexicon.** Compiled by H. G. LIDDELL, D.D. Dean of Christ Church, and R. SCOTT, D.D. Dean of Rochester. Sixth Edition. Crown 4to. price 36s.

**A Lexicon, Greek and English,** abridged for Schools from LIDDELL and SCOTT's *Greek-English Lexicon*. Twelfth Edition. Square 12mo. 7s. 6d.

**A Practical Dictionary of the** French and English Languages. By Professor LÉON CONTANSEAU, many years French Examiner for Military and Civil Appointments, &c. New Edition, carefully revised. Post 8vo. 10s. 6d.

**Contanseau's Pocket Dictionary,** French and English, abridged from the Practical Dictionary, by the Author. New Edition. 18mo. price 3s. 6d.

**A Sanskrit-English Dictionary.** The Sanskrit words printed both in the original Devanagari and in Roman letters; with References to the Best Editions of Sanskrit Authors, and with Etymologies and comparisons of Cognate Words chiefly in Greek, Latin, Gothic, and Anglo-Saxon. Compiled by T. BENFEY. 8vo. 52s. 6d.

**New Practical Dictionary of the** German Language; German-English, and English-German. By the Rev. W. L. BLACKLEY, M.A. and Dr. CARL MARTIN FRIEDLÄNDER. Post 8vo. 7s. 6d.

**Staff College Essays.** By Lieutenant EVELYN BARING, Royal Artillery. 8vo. with Two Maps, 8s. 6d.

---

## *Miscellaneous Works* and *Popular Metaphysics.*

**The Essays and Contributions of** A. K. H. B. Author of 'The Recreations of a Country Parson.' Uniform Editions:—

**Recreations of a Country Parson.** FIRST and SECOND SERIES, 3s. 6d. each.

**The Commonplace Philosopher in Town and Country.** Crown 8vo. 3s. 6d.

**Leisure Hours in Town;** Essays Consolatory, Æsthetical, Moral, Social, and Domestic. Crown 8vo. 3s. 6d.

**The Autumn Holidays of a Country Parson.** Crown 8vo. 3s. 6d.

**The Graver Thoughts of a Country Parson.** FIRST and SECOND SERIES, crown 8vo. 3s. 6d. each.

**Critical Essays of a Country Parson,** selected from Essays contributed to *Fraser's Magazine*. Crown 8vo. 3s. 6d.

**Sunday Afternoons at the Parish Church of a Scottish University City.** Crown 8vo. 3s. 6d.

**Lessons of Middle Age,** with some Account of various Cities and Men. Crown 8vo. 3s. 6d.

**Counsel and Comfort Spoken from a City Pulpit.** Crown 8vo. 3s. 6d.

**Changed Aspects of Unchanged Truths;** Memorials of St. Andrews Sundays. Crown 8vo. 3s. 6d.

**Present-Day Thoughts;** Memorials of St. Andrews Sundays. Crown 8vo. 3s. 6d.

**Short Studies on Great Subjects.** By JAMES ANTHONY FROUDE, M.A. late Fellow of Exeter College, Oxford. Third Edition. 8vo. 12s.

**Lord Macaulay's Miscellaneous Writings:—**
LIBRARY EDITION, 2 vols. 8vo. Portrait, 21s.
PEOPLE'S EDITION, 1 vol. crown 8vo. 4s. 6d.

**The Rev. Sydney Smith's Miscellaneous Works;** including his Contributions to the *Edinburgh Review*. 1 vol. crown 8vo. 6s.

**The Wit and Wisdom of the Rev.** SYDNEY SMITH: a Selection of the most memorable Passages in his Writings and Conversation. Crown 8vo. 3s. 6d.

**The Silver Store.** Collected from Mediæval Christian and Jewish Mines. By the Rev. S. BARING-GOULD, M.A. Crown 8vo. 3s. 6d.

**Traces of History in the Names** of Places; with a Vocabulary of the Roots out of which Names of Places in England and Wales are formed. By FLAVELL EDMUNDS. Crown 8vo. 7s. 6d.

**The Eclipse of Faith;** or, a Visit to a Religious Sceptic. By HENRY ROGERS. Twelfth Edition. Fcp. 5s.

**Defence of the Eclipse of Faith,** by its Author. Third Edition. Fcp. 3s. 6d.

**Selections from the Correspondence** of R. E. H. Greyson. By the same Author. Third Edition. Crown 8vo. 7s. 6d.

**Families of Speech,** Four Lectures delivered at the Royal Institution of Great Britain. By the Rev. F. W. FARRAR, M.A. F.R.S. Post 8vo. with 2 Maps, 5s. 6d.

**Chips from a German Workshop;** being Essays on the Science of Religion, and on Mythology, Traditions, and Customs. By MAX MÜLLER, M.A. &c. Foreign Member of the French Institute. 3 vols. 8vo. £2.

**Word Gossip;** a Series of Familiar Essays on Words and their Peculiarities. By the Rev. W. L. BLACKLEY, M.A. Fcp. 8vo. 5s.

**An Introduction to Mental Philosophy,** on the Inductive Method. By J. D. MORELL, M.A. LL.D. 8vo. 12s.

**Elements of Psychology,** containing the Analysis of the Intellectual Powers. By the same Author. Post 8vo. 7s. 6d.

**The Secret of Hegel:** being the Hegelian System in Origin, Principle, Form, and Matter. By JAMES HUTCHISON STIRLING. 2 vols. 8vo. 28s.

**Sir William Hamilton;** being the Philosophy of Perception: an Analysis. By the same Author. 8vo. 5s.

**The Senses and the Intellect.** By ALEXANDER BAIN, LL.D. Prof. of Logic in the Univ. of Aberdeen. Third Edition. 8vo. 15s.

**The Emotions and the Will,** by the same Author. Second Edition. 8vo. 15s.

**On the Study of Character,** including an Estimate of Phrenology. By the same Author. 8vo. 9s.

**Mental and Moral Science:** a Compendium of Psychology and Ethics. By the same Author. Second Edition. Crown 8vo. 10s. 6d.

**Strong and Free;** or, First Steps towards Social Science. By the Author of 'My Life and What shall I do with it?' 8vo. 10s. 6d.

**The Philosophy of Necessity;** or, Natural Law as applicable to Mental, Moral, and Social Science. By CHARLES BRAY. Second Edition. 8vo. 9s.

**The Education of the Feelings and Affections.** By the same Author. Third Edition. 8vo. 3s. 6d.

**On Force, its Mental and Moral Correlates.** By the same Author. 8vo. 5s.

**Time and Space;** a Metaphysical Essay. By SHADWORTH H. HODGSON. (This work covers the whole ground of Speculative Philosophy.) 8vo. price 16s.

**The Theory of Practice;** an Ethical Inquiry. By the same Author. (This work, in conjunction with the foregoing, completes a system of Philosophy.) 2 vols. 8vo. price 24s.

**A Treatise on Human Nature;** being an Attempt to Introduce the Experimental Method of Reasoning into Moral Subjects. By DAVID HUME. Edited, with Notes, &c. by T. H. GREEN, Fellow, and T. H. GROSE, late Scholar, of Balliol College, Oxford. [*In the press.*

**Essays Moral, Political, and Literary.** By DAVID HUME. By the same Editors. [*In the press.*

\*\*\* The above will form a new edition of DAVID HUME's *Philosophical Works*, complete in Four Volumes, but to be had in Two separate Sections as announced.

## Astronomy, Meteorology, Popular Geography, &c.

**Outlines of Astronomy.** By Sir J. F. W. HERSCHEL, Bart. M.A. New Edition, revised; with Plates and Woodcuts. 8vo. 18s.

**Other Worlds than Ours;** the Plurality of Worlds Studied under the Light of Recent Scientific Researches. By R. A. PROCTOR, B.A. F.R.A.S. Second Edition, revised and enlarged; with 14 Illustrations. Crown 8vo. 10s. 6d.

**The Sun; Ruler, Light, Fire, and** Life of the Planetary System. By the same Author. With 10 Plates (7 coloured) and 107 Woodcuts. Crown 8vo. price 14s.

**Saturn and its System.** By the same Author. 8vo. with 14 Plates, 14s.

**The Handbook of the Stars.** By the same Author. Square fcp. 8vo. with 3 Maps, price 5s.

**Celestial Objects for Common Telescopes.** By T. W. WEBB, M.A. F.R.A.S. Second Edition, revised and enlarged, with Map of the Moon and Woodcuts. 16mo. price 7s. 6d.

**Navigation and Nautical Astronomy** (Practical, Theoretical, Scientific) for the use of Students and Practical Men. By J. MERRIFIELD, F.R.A.S. and H. EVERS. 8vo. 14s.

**A General Dictionary of Geography,** Descriptive, Physical, Statistical, and Historical; forming a complete Gazetteer of the World. By A. KEITH JOHNSTON, F.R.S.E. New Edition. 8vo. price 31s. 6d.

**M'Culloch's Dictionary, Geographical,** Statistical, and Historical, of the various Countries, Places, and principal Natural Objects in the World. Revised Edition, with the Statistical Information throughout brought up to the latest returns By FREDERICK MARTIN. 4 vols. 8vo. with coloured Maps, £4 4s.

**A Manual of Geography,** Physical, Industrial, and Political. By W. HUGHES, F.R.G.S. Prof. of Geog. in King's Coll. and in Queen's Coll. Lond. With 6 Maps. Fcp. 7s. 6d.

**The States of the River Plate:** their Industries and Commerce, Sheep Farming, Sheep Breeding, Cattle Feeding, and Meat Preserving; the Employment of Capital, Land and Stock and their Values, Labour and its Remuneration. By WILFRID LATHAM, Buenos Ayres. Second Edition. 8vo. 12s.

**Maunder's Treasury of Geography,** Physical, Historical, Descriptive, and Political. Edited by W. HUGHES, F.R.G.S. With 7 Maps and 16 Plates. Fcp. 6s.

---

## Natural History and Popular Science.

**Ganot's Elementary Treatise on Physics,** Experimental and Applied, for the use of Colleges and Schools. Translated and Edited with the Author's sanction by E. ATKINSON, Ph.D. F.C.S. New Edition, revised and enlarged; with a Coloured Plate and 620 Woodcuts. Post 8vo. 15s.

**The Elements of Physics or Natural Philosophy.** By NEIL ARNOTT, M.D. F.R.S. Physician-Extraordinary to the Queen. Sixth Edition, re-written and completed. 2 Parts, 8vo. 21s.

**The Forces of the Universe.** By GEORGE BERWICK, M.D. Post 8vo. 5s.

**Dove's Law of Storms,** considered in connexion with the ordinary Movements of the Atmosphere. Translated by R. H. SCOTT, M.A. T.C.D. 8vo. 10s. 6d.

**Sound:** a Course of Eight Lectures delivered at the Royal Institution of Great Britain. By Professor JOHN TYNDALL, LL.D. F.R.S. New Edition, with Portrait and Woodcuts. Crown 8vo. 9s.

**Heat a Mode of Motion.** By Professor JOHN TYNDALL, LL.D. F.R.S. Fourth Edition. Crown 8vo. with Woodcuts, price 10s. 6d.

**Researches on Diamagnetism** and Magne-Crystallic Action; including the Question of Diamagnetic Polarity. By Professor TYNDALL. With 6 Plates and many Woodcuts. 8vo. 14s.

**Notes of a Course of Nine Lectures** on Light, delivered at the Royal Institution, A.D. 1869. By Professor TYNDALL. Crown 8vo. 1s. sewed, or 1s. 6d. cloth.

**Notes of a Course of Seven Lectures** on Electrical Phenomena and Theories, delivered at the Royal Institution, A.D. 1870. By Professor TYNDALL. Crown 8vo. 1s. sewed, or 1s. 6d. cloth.

**Professor Tyndall's Essays** on the Use and Limit of the Imagination in Science. Being the Second Edition, with Additions, of a Discourse on the Scientific Use of the Imagination. 8vo. 3s.

**Light**: its Influence on Life and Health. By FORBES WINSLOW, M.D. D.C.L. Oxon. (Hon.) Fcp. 8vo. 6s.

**A Treatise on Electricity**, in Theory and Practice. By A. DE LA RIVE, Prof. in the Academy of Geneva. Translated by C. V. WALKER, F.R.S. 3 vols. 8vo. with Woodcuts, £3 13s.

**The Correlation of Physical Forces.** By W. R. GROVE, Q.C. V.P.R.S. Fifth Edition, revised, and Augmented by a Discourse on Continuity. 8vo. 10s. 6d. The *Discourse*, separately, price 2s. 6d.

**The Beginning: its When and its How.** By MUNGO PONTON, F.R.S.E. Post 8vo. with very numerous Illustrations.

**Manual of Geology.** By S. HAUGHTON, M.D. F.R.S. Fellow of Trin. Coll. and Prof. of Geol. in the Univ. of Dublin. Second Edition, with 66 Woodcuts. Fcp. 7s. 6d.

**Van Der Hoeven's Handbook of** ZOOLOGY. Translated from the Second Dutch Edition by the Rev. W. CLARK, M.D. F.R.S. 2 vols. 8vo. with 24 Plates of Figures, 60s.

**Professor Owen's Lectures on** the Comparative Anatomy and Physiology of the Invertebrate Animals. Second Edition, with 235 Woodcuts. 8vo. 21s.

**The Comparative Anatomy and** Physiology of the Vertebrate Animals. By RICHARD OWEN, F.R.S. D.C.L. With 1,472 Woodcuts. 3 vols. 8vo. £3 13s. 6d.

**The Origin of Civilisation and** the Primitive Condition of Man ; Mental and Social Condition of Savages. By Sir JOHN LUBBOCK, Bart. M.P. F.R.S. Second Edition, revised, with 25 Woodcuts. 8vo. price 16s.

**The Primitive Inhabitants of** Scandinavia. Containing a Description of the Implements, Dwellings, Tombs, and Mode of Living of the Savages in the North of Europe during the Stone Age. By SVEN NILSSON. 8vo. Plates and Woodcuts, 18s.

**Homes without Hands**: a Description of the Habitations of Animals, classed according to their Principle of Construction. By Rev. J. G. WOOD, M.A. F.L.S. With about 140 Vignettes on Wood. 8vo. 21s.

**Bible Animals;** being a Description of Every Living Creature mentioned in the Scriptures, from the Ape to the Coral. By the Rev. J. G. WOOD, M.A. F.L.S. With about 100 Vignettes on Wood. 8vo. 21s.

**The Harmonies of Nature and** Unity of Creation. By Dr. G. HARTWIG. 8vo. with numerous Illustrations, 18s.

**The Sea and its Living Wonders.** By the same Author. Third Edition, enlarged. 8vo. with many Illustrations, 21s.

**The Tropical World.** By the same Author. With 8 Chromoxylographs and 172 Woodcuts. 8vo. 21s.

**The Polar World:** a Popular Description of Man and Nature in the Arctic and Antarctic Regions of the Globe. By the same Author. With 8 Chromoxylographs, 3 Maps, and 85 Woodcuts. 8vo. 21s.

**A Familiar History of Birds.** By E. STANLEY, D.D. late Lord Bishop of Norwich. Fcp. with Woodcuts, 3s. 6d.

**Kirby and Spence's Introduction** to Entomology, or Elements of the Natural History of Insects. Crown 8vo. 5s.

**Maunder's Treasury of Natural** History, or Popular Dictionary of Zoology. Revised and corrected by T. S. COBBOLD, M.D. Fcp. with 900 Woodcuts, 6s.

**The Elements of Botany for** Families and Schools. Tenth Edition, revised by THOMAS MOORE, F.L.S. Fcp. with 154 Woodcuts, 2s. 6d.

**The Treasury of Botany, or** Popular Dictionary of the Vegetable Kingdom; with which is incorporated a Glossary of Botanical Terms. Edited by J. LINDLEY, F.R.S. and T. MOORE, F.L.S. assisted by eminent Contributors. Pp. 1,274, with 274 Woodcuts and 20 Steel Plates. TWO PARTS, fcp. 8vo. 12s.

**The British Flora;** comprising the Phænogamous or Flowering Plants and the Ferns. By Sir W. J. HOOKER, K.H. and G. A. WALKER-ARNOTT, LL.D. 12mo. with 12 Plates, 14s.

**The Rose Amateur's Guide.** By THOMAS RIVERS. New Edition. Fcp. 4s.

**Loudon's Encyclopædia of Plants;** comprising the Specific Character, Description, Culture, History, &c. of all the Plants found in Great Britain. With upwards of 12,000 Woodcuts. 8vo. 42s.

**Maunder's Scientific and Literary Treasury;** a Popular Encyclopædia of Science, Literature, and Art. New Edition, thoroughly revised and in great part re-written, with above 1,000 new articles, by J. Y. JOHNSON, Corr. M.Z.S. Fcp. 6s.

**A Dictionary of Science, Literature, and Art.** Fourth Edition, re-edited by the late W. T. BRANDE (the Author) and GEORGE W. COX, M.A. 3 vols. medium 8vo. price 63s. cloth.

## *Chemistry, Medicine, Surgery,* and *the Allied Sciences.*

**A Dictionary of Chemistry and** the Allied Branches of other Sciences. By HENRY WATTS, F.C.S. assisted by eminent Scientific and Practical Chemists. 5 vols. medium 8vo. price £7 3s.

**Elements of Chemistry, Theoretical and Practical.** By WILLIAM A. MILLER, M.D. LL.D. Professor of Chemistry, King's College, London. Fourth Edition. 3 vols. 8vo. £3.
    PART I. CHEMICAL PHYSICS, 15s.
    PART II. INORGANIC CHEMISTRY, 21s.
    PART III. ORGANIC CHEMISTRY, 24s.

**A Manual of Chemistry,** Descriptive and Theoretical. By WILLIAM ODLING, M.B. F.R.S. PART I. 8vo. 9s. PART II. nearly ready.

**A Course of Practical Chemistry,** for the use of Medical Students. By W. ODLING, M.B. F.R.S. New Edition, with 70 new Woodcuts. Crown 8vo. 7s. 6d.

**Outlines of Chemistry;** or, Brief Notes of Chemical Facts. By the same Author. Crown 8vo. 7s. 6d.

**Lectures on Animal Chemistry** Delivered at the Royal College of Physicians in 1865. By the same Author. Crown 8vo. 4s. 6d.

**Lectures on the Chemical Changes of Carbon,** delivered at the Royal Institution of Great Britain. By the same Author. Crown 8vo. 4s. 6d.

**Chemical Notes for the Lecture Room.** By THOMAS WOOD, F.C.S. 2 vols. crown 8vo. I. on Heat, &c. price 3s. 6d. II. on the Metals, price 5s.

**A Treatise on Medical Electricity,** Theoretical and Practical; and its Use in the Treatment of Paralysis, Neuralgia, and other Diseases. By JULIUS ALTHAUS, M.D. &c. Second Edition, revised and partly re-written; with Plate and 62 Woodcuts. Post 8vo. price 15s.

**The Diagnosis, Pathology, and** Treatment of Diseases of Women; including the Diagnosis of Pregnancy. By GRAILY HEWITT, M.D. &c. President of the Obstetrical Society of London. Second Edition, enlarged; with 116 Woodcuts. 8vo. 24s.

**Lectures on the Diseases of Infancy and Childhood.** By CHARLES WEST, M.D. &c. Fifth Edition. 8vo. 16s.

**On the Surgical Treatment of** Children's Diseases. By T. HOLMES, M.A. &c. late Surgeon to the Hospital for Sick Children. Second Edition, with 9 Plates and 112 Woodcuts. 8vo. 21s.

**A System of Surgery, Theoretical** and Practical, in Treatises by Various Authors. Edited by T. HOLMES, M.A. &c. Surgeon and Lecturer on Surgery at St. George's Hospital, and Surgeon-in-Chief to the Metropolitan Police. Second Edition, thoroughly revised, with numerous Illustrations. 5 vols. 8vo. £5 5s.

**Lectures on the Principles and** Practice of Physic. By Sir THOMAS WATSON, Bart. M.D. Physician-in-Ordinary to the Queen. New Edition in the press.

**Lectures on Surgical Pathology.** By JAMES PAGET, F.R.S. Third Edition, revised and re-edited by the Author and Professor W. TURNER, M.B. 8vo. with 131 Woodcuts, 21s.

**Cooper's Dictionary of Practical** Surgery and Encyclopædia of Surgical Science. New Edition, brought down to the present time. By S. A. LANE, Surgeon to St. Mary's Hospital, &c. assisted by various Eminent Surgeons. VOL. II. 8vo. completing the work. [*Early* in 1871.

**On Chronic Bronchitis,** especially as connected with Gout, Emphysema, and Diseases of the Heart. By E. HEADLAM GREENHOW, M.D. F.R.C.P. &c. 8vo. 7s. 6d.

**The Climate of the South of** France as Suited to Invalids; with Notices of Mediterranean and other Winter Stations. By C. T. WILLIAMS, M.A. M.D. Oxon. Assistant-Physician to the Hospital for Consumption at Brompton. Second Edition. Crown 8vo. 6s.

**Pulmonary Consumption;** its Nature, Treatment, and Duration exemplified by an Analysis of One Thousand Cases selected from upwards of Twenty Thousand. By C. J. B. WILLIAMS, M.D. F.R.S. Consulting Physician to the Hospital for Consumption at Brompton; and C. T. WILLIAMS, M.A. M.D. Oxon.
[*Nearly ready.*

**Clinical Lectures on Diseases of** the Liver, Jaundice, and Abdominal Dropsy. By C. MURCHISON, M.D. Physician and Lecturer on the Practice of Medicine, Middlesex Hospital. Post 8vo. with 25 Woodcuts, 10s. 6d.

**Anatomy, Descriptive and Surgical.** By HENRY GRAY, F.R.S. With about 410 Woodcuts from Dissections. Fifth Edition, by T. HOLMES, M.A. Cantab. With a New Introduction by the Editor. Royal 8vo. 28s.

**Clinical Notes on Diseases of** the Larynx, investigated and treated with the assistance of the Laryngoscope. By W. MARCET, M.D. F.R.S. Crown 8vo. with 5 Lithographs, 6s.

**The House I Live in;** or, Popular Illustrations of the Structure and Functions of the Human Body. Edited by T. G. GIRTIN. New Edition, with 25 Woodcuts. 16mo. price 2s. 6d.

**Outlines of Physiology,** Human and Comparative. By JOHN MARSHALL, F.R.C.S. Professor of Surgery in University College, London, and Surgeon to the University College Hospital. 2 vols. crown 8vo. with 122 Woodcuts, 32s.

**Physiological Anatomy and Physiology** of Man. By the late R. B. TODD, M.D. F.R.S. and W. BOWMAN, F.R.S. of King's College. With numerous Illustrations. VOL. II. 8vo. 25s.
VOL. I. New Edition by Dr. LIONEL S. BEALE, F.R.S. in course of publication; PART I. with 8 Plates, 7s. 6d.

**Copland's Dictionary of Practical** Medicine, abridged from the larger work, and throughout brought down to the present state of Medical Science. 8vo. 36s.

**A Manual of Materia Medica** and Therapeutics, abridged from Dr. PEREIRA's *Elements* by F. J. FARRE, M.D. assisted by R. BENTLEY, M.R.C.S. and by R. WARINGTON, F.R.S. 1 vol. 8vo. with 90 Woodcuts, 21s.

**Thomson's Conspectus of the** British Pharmacopœia. Twenty-fifth Edition, corrected by E. LLOYD BIRKETT, M.D. 18mo. 6s.

**Essays on Physiological Subjects.** By GILBERT W. CHILD, M.A. F.L.S. F.C.S. Second Edition. Crown 8vo. with Woodcuts, 7s. 6d.

## *The Fine Arts,* and *Illustrated Editions.*

**In Fairyland;** Pictures from the Elf-World. By RICHARD DOYLE. With a Poem by W. ALLINGHAM. With Sixteen Plates, containing Thirty-six Designs printed in Colours. Folio, 31s. 6d.

**Life of John Gibson, R.A.** Sculptor. Edited by Lady EASTLAKE. 8vo. 10s. 6d.

**Materials for a History of Oil** Painting. By Sir CHARLES LOCKE EASTLAKE, sometime President of the Royal Academy. 2 vols. 8vo. 30s.

**Albert Durer, his Life and** Works; including Autobiographical Papers and Complete Catalogues. By WILLIAM B. SCOTT. With Six Etchings by the Author and other Illustrations. 8vo. 16s.

**Half-Hour Lectures on the History** and Practice of the Fine and Ornamental Arts. By. W. B. SCOTT. Second Edition. Crown 8vo. with 50 Woodcut Illustrations, 8s. 6d.

**The Lord's Prayer Illustrated** by F. R. PICKERSGILL, R.A. and HENRY ALFORD, D.D. Dean of Canterbury. Imp. 4to. 21s.

**The Chorale Book for England:** the Hymns Translated by Miss C. WINKWORTH; the Tunes arranged by Prof. W. S. BENNETT and OTTO GOLDSCHMIDT. Fcp. 4to. 12s. 6d.

**Six Lectures on Harmony.** Delivered at the Royal Institution of Great Britain. By G. A. MACFARREN. 8vo. 10s. 6d.

**Lyra Germanica,** the Christian Year. Translated by CATHERINE WINKWORTH; with 125 Illustrations on Wood drawn by J. LEIGHTON, F.S.A. Quarto, 21s.

**Lyra Germanica.** the Christian Life. Translated by CATHERINE WINKWORTH; with about 200 Woodcut Illustrations by J. LEIGHTON, F.S.A. and other Artists. Quarto, 21s.

**The New Testament,** illustrated with Wood Engravings after the Early Masters, chiefly of the Italian School. Crown 4to. 63s. cloth, gilt top ; or £5 5s. morocco.

**The Life of Man Symbolised by** the Months of the Year in their Seasons and Phases. Text selected by RICHARD PIGOT. 25 Illustrations on Wood from Original Designs by JOHN LEIGHTON, F.S.A. Quarto, 42s.

**Cats' and Farlie's Moral Emblems**; with Aphorisms, Adages, and Proverbs of all Nations: comprising 121 Illustrations on Wood by J. LEIGHTON, F.S.A. with an appropriate Text by R. PIGOT. Imperial 8vo. 31s. 6d.

**Shakspeare's Midsummer Night's Dream,** illustrated with 24 Silhouettes or Shadow Pictures by P. KONEWKA, engraved on Wood by A. VOGEL. Folio, 31s. 6d.

**Sacred and Legendary Art.** By Mrs. JAMESON. 6 vols. square crown 8vo. price £5 15s. 6d.

**Legends of the Saints and Martyrs.** Fifth Edition, with 19 Etchings and 187 Woodcuts. 2 vols. price 31s. 6d.

**Legends of the Monastic Orders.** Third Edition, with 11 Etchings and 88 Woodcuts. 1 vol. price 21s.

**Legends of the Madonna.** Third Edition, with 27 Etchings and 165 Woodcuts. 1 vol. price 21s.

**The History of Our Lord,** with that of His Types and Precursors. Completed by Lady EASTLAKE. Revised Edition, with 13 Etchings and 281 Woodcuts. 2 vols. price 42s.

## The Useful Arts, Manufactures, &c.

**Gwilt's Encyclopædia of Architecture,** with above 1,600 Woodcuts. Fifth Edition, with Alterations and considerable Additions, by WYATT PAPWORTH. 8vo. 52s. 6d.

**A Manual of Architecture**: being a Concise History and Explanation of the principal Styles of European Architecture, Ancient, Mediæval, and Renaissance ; with their Chief Variations and a Glossary of Technical Terms. By THOMAS MITCHELL. With 150 Woodcuts. Crown 8vo. 10s. 6d.

**Italian Sculptors**: being a History of Sculpture in Northern, Southern, and Eastern Italy. By C. C. PERKINS. With 30 Etchings and 13 Wood Engravings. Imperial 8vo. 42s.

**Tuscan Sculptors, their Lives,** Works, and Times. By the same Author. With 45 Etchings and 28 Woodcuts from Original Drawings and Photographs. 2 vols. imperial 8vo. 63s.

**Hints on Household Taste in** Furniture, Upholstery, and other Details. By CHARLES L. EASTLAKE, Architect. Second Edition, with about 90 Illustrations. Square crown 8vo. 18s.

**The Engineer's Handbook ;** explaining the principles which should guide the young Engineer in the Construction of Machinery. By C. S. LOWNDES. Post 8vo. 5s.

**Lathes and Turning, Simple, Mechanical, and Ornamental.** By W. HENRY NORTHCOTT. With about 240 Illustrations on Steel and Wood. 8vo. 18s.

**Principles of Mechanism,** designed for the use of Students in the Universities, and for Engineering Students generally. By R. WILLIS, M.A. F.R.S. &c. Jacksonian Professor in the Univ. of Cambridge. Second Edition, enlarged ; with 374 Woodcuts. 8vo. 18s.

**Handbook of Practical Telegraphy,** published with the sanction of the Chairman and Directors of the Electric and International Telegraph Company, and adopted by the Department of Telegraphs for India. By R. S. CULLEY. Third Edition. 8vo. 12s. 6d.

**Ure's Dictionary of Arts, Manufactures, and Mines.** Sixth Edition, rewritten and greatly enlarged by ROBERT HUNT, F.R.S. assisted by numerous Contributors. With 2,000 Woodcuts. 3 vols. medium 8vo. £4 14s. 6d.

**Treatise on Mills and Millwork.** By Sir W. FAIRBAIRN, Bart. With 18 Plates and 322 Woodcuts. 2 vols. 8vo. 32s.

**Useful Information for Engineers.** By the same Author. FIRST, SECOND, and THIRD SERIES, with many Plates and Woodcuts. 3 vols. crown 8vo. 10s. 6d. each.

**The Application of Cast and Wrought Iron to Building Purposes.** By the same Author. Fourth Edition, with 6 Plates and 118 Woodcuts. 8vo. 16s.

**Iron Ship Building, its History** and Progress, as comprised in a Series of Experimental Researches. By W. FAIRBAIRN, Bart. F.R.S. With 4 Plates and 130 Woodcuts, 8vo. 18s.

**Encyclopædia of Civil Engineering,** Historical, Theoretical, and Practical. By E. CRESY, C.E. With above 3,000 Woodcuts. 8vo. 42s.

**A Treatise on the Steam Engine,** in its various Applications to Mines, Mills, Steam Navigation, Railways, and Agriculture. By J. BOURNE, C.E. New Edition; with Portrait, 37 Plates, and 546 Woodcuts. 4to. 42s.

**Catechism of the Steam Engine,** in its various Applications to Mines, Mills, Steam Navigation, Railways, and Agriculture. By JOHN BOURNE, C.E. New Edition, with 89 Woodcuts. Fcp. 6s.

**Recent Improvements in the Steam-Engine.** By JOHN BOURNE, C.E. being a SUPPLEMENT to his 'Catechism of the Steam-Engine.' New Edition, including many New Examples, with 124 Woodcuts. Fcp. 8vo. 6s.

**Bourne's Examples of Modern Steam, Air, and Gas Engines** of the most Approved Types, as employed for Pumping, for Driving Machinery, for Locomotion, and for Agriculture, minutely and practically described. In course of publication, to be completed in Twenty-four Parts, price 2s. 6d. each, forming One Volume, with about 50 Plates and 400 Woodcuts.

**A Treatise on the Screw Propeller,** Screw Vessels, and Screw Engines, as adapted for purposes of Peace and War. By JOHN BOURNE, C.E. Third Edition, with 54 Plates and 287 Woodcuts. Quarto, 63s.

**Handbook of the Steam Engine.** By JOHN BOURNE, C.E. forming a KEY to the Author's Catechism of the Steam Engine. With 67 Woodcuts. Fcp. 9s.

**A History of the Machine-Wrought Hosiery and Lace Manufactures.** By WILLIAM FELKIN, F.L.S. F.S.S. With several Illustrations. Royal 8vo. 21s.

**Mitchell's Manual of Practical Assaying.** Third Edition for the most part re-written, with all the recent Discoveries incorporated. By W. CROOKES, F.R.S. With 188 Woodcuts. 8vo. 28s.

**Reimann's Handbook of Aniline** and its Derivatives; a Treatise on the Manufacture of Aniline and Aniline Colours. Revised and edited by WILLIAM CROOKES, F.R.S. 8vo. with 5 Woodcuts, 10s. 6d.

**On the Manufacture of Beet-Root Sugar** in England and Ireland. By WILLIAM CROOKES, F.R.S. With 11 Woodcuts. 8vo. 8s. 6d.

**Practical Treatise on Metallurgy,** adapted from the last German Edition of Professor KERL'S *Metallurgy* by W. CROOKES, F.R.S. &c. and E. RÖHRIG, Ph.D. M.E. 3 vols. 8vo. with 625 Woodcuts, price £4 19s.

**The Art of Perfumery;** the History and Theory of Odours, and the Methods of Extracting the Aromas of Plants. By Dr. PIESSE, F.C.S. Third Edition, with 53 Woodcuts. Crown 8vo. 10s. 6d.

**Chemical, Natural, and Physical Magic,** for Juveniles during the Holidays. By the same Author. With 38 Woodcuts. Fcp. 6s.

**Loudon's Encyclopædia of Agriculture:** comprising the Laying-out, Improvement, and Management of Landed Property, and the Cultivation and Economy of the Productions of Agriculture. With 1,100 Woodcuts. 8vo. 21s.

**Loudon's Encyclopædia of Gardening:** comprising the Theory and Practice of Horticulture, Floriculture, Arboriculture, and Landscape Gardening. With 1,000 Woodcuts. 8vo. 21s.

**Bayldon's Art of Valuing Rents** and Tillages, and Claims of Tenants upon Quitting Farms, both at Michaelmas and Lady-Day. Eighth Edition, revised by J. C. MORTON. 8vo. 10s. 6d.

## Religious and Moral Works.

**An Exposition of the 39 Articles,** Historical and Doctrinal. By E. HAROLD BROWNE, D.D. Lord Bishop of Ely. Eighth Edition. 8vo. 16s.

**Examination-Questions on Bishop Browne's Exposition of the Articles.** By the Rev. J. GORLE, M.A. Fcp. 3s. 6d.

**The Life and Epistles of St. Paul.** By the Rev. W. J. CONYBEARE, M.A. and the Very Rev. J. S. HOWSON, D.D. Dean of Chester.

LIBRARY EDITION, with all the Original Illustrations, Maps, Landscapes on Steel, Woodcuts, &c. 2 vols. 4to. 48s.

INTERMEDIATE EDITION, with a Selection of Maps, Plates, and Woodcuts. 2 vols. square crown 8vo. 31s. 6d.

STUDENT'S EDITION, revised and condensed, with 46 Illustrations and Maps. 1 vol. crown 8vo. 9s.

**The Voyage and Shipwreck of St. Paul;** with Dissertations on the Ships and Navigation of the Ancients. By JAMES SMITH, F.R.S. Crown 8vo. Charts, 10s. 6d.

**Evidence of the Truth of the** Christian Religion derived from the Literal Fulfilment of Prophecy. By ALEXANDER KEITH, D.D. 37th Edition, with numerous Plates, in square 8vo. 12s. 6d.; also the 39th Edition, in post 8vo. with 5 Plates, 6s.

**The History and Destiny of the World** and of the Church, according to Scripture. By the same Author. Square 8vo. with 40 Illustrations, 10s.

**The History and Literature of** the Israelites, according to the Old Testament and the Apocrypha. By C. DE ROTHSCHILD and A. DE ROTHSCHILD. With 2 Maps. 2 vols. post 8vo. price 12s. 6d.
VOL. I. *The Historical Books,* 7s. 6d.
VOL. II. *The Prophetic and Poetical Writings,* price 5s.

**Ewald's History of Israel to the** Death of Moses. Translated from the German. Edited, with a Preface and an Appendix, by RUSSELL MARTINEAU, M.A. Second Edition. 2 vols. 8vo. 24s.

**History of the Karaite Jews.** By WILLIAM HARRIS RULE, D.D. Post 8vo. price 7s. 6d.

**The Life of Margaret Mary** Hallahan, better known in the religious world by the name of Mother Margaret. By her RELIGIOUS CHILDREN. Second Edition. 8vo. with Portrait, 10s.

**The See of Rome in the Middle** Ages. By the Rev. OSWALD J. REICHEL, B.C.L. and M.A. 8vo. 18s.

**The Evidence for the Papacy** as derived from the Holy Scriptures and from Primitive Antiquity. By the Hon. COLIN LINDSAY. 8vo. 12s. 6d.

**The Pontificate of Pius the Ninth;** being the Third Edition, enlarged and continued, of 'Rome and its Ruler.' By J. F. MAGUIRE, M.P. Post 8vo. Portrait, price 12s. 6d.

**Ignatius Loyola and the Early** Jesuits. By STEWART ROSE. New Edition, in the press.

**An Introduction to the Study of** the New Testament, Critical, Exegetical, and Theological. By the Rev. S. DAVIDSON, D.D. LL.D. 2 vols. 8vo. 30s.

**A Critical and Grammatical Commentary on St. Paul's Epistles.** By C. J. ELLICOTT, D.D. Lord Bishop of Gloucester and Bristol. 8vo.
Galatians, Fourth Edition, 8s. 6d.
Ephesians, Fourth Edition, 8s. 6d.
Pastoral Epistles, Fourth Edition, 10s. 6d.
Philippians, Colossians, and Philemon, Third Edition, 10s. 6d.
Thessalonians, Third Edition, 7s. 6d.

**Historical Lectures on the Life of** Our Lord Jesus Christ: being the Hulsean Lectures for 1859. By C. J. ELLICOTT, D.D. Lord Bishop of Gloucester and Bristol. Fifth Edition. 8vo. 12s.

**The Greek Testament; with Notes,** Grammatical and Exegetical. By the Rev. W. WEBSTER, M.A. and the Rev. W. F. WILKINSON, M.A. 2 vols. 8vo. £2 4s.

**Horne's Introduction to the Critical Study and Knowledge of the Holy Scriptures.** Twelfth Edition; with 4 Maps and 22 Woodcuts and Facsimiles. 4 vols. 8vo. 42s.

**Compendious Introduction to the** Study of the Bible. Edited by the Rev. JOHN AYRE, M.A. With Maps, &c. Post 8vo. 6s.

**The Treasury of Bible Knowledge;** being a Dictionary of the Books, Persons, Places, Events, and other Matters of which mention is made in Holy Scripture. By Rev. J. AYRE, M.A. With Maps, 15 Plates, and numerous Woodcuts. Fcp. 6s.

**Every-day Scripture Difficulties** explained and illustrated. By J. E. PRESCOTT, M.A. VOL. I. *Matthew* and *Mark*; VOL. II. *Luke* and *John*. 2 vols. 8vo. price 9s. each.

**The Pentateuch and Book of** Joshua Critically Examined. By the Right Rev. J. W. COLENSO, D.D. Lord Bishop of Natal. Crown 8vo. price 6s.

**The Four Cardinal Virtues** (Fortitude, Justice, Prudence, Temperance) in relation to the Public and Private Life of Catholics: Six Sermons for the Day. With Preface, Appendices, &c. By the Rev. ORBY SHIPLEY, M.A. Crown 8vo. with Frontispiece, 7s. 6d.

**The Formation of Christendom.** By T. W. ALLIES. PARTS I. and II. 8vo. price 12s. each.

**Four Discourses of Chrysostom,** chiefly on the parable of the Rich Man and Lazarus. Translated by F. ALLEN, B.A. Crown 8vo. 3s. 6d.

**Christendom's Divisions;** a Philosophical Sketch of the Divisions of the Christian Family in East and West. By EDMUND S. FFOULKES. Post 8vo. 7s. 6d.

**Christendom's Divisions,** PART II. *Greeks and Latins.* By the same Author. Post 8vo. 15s.

**The Hidden Wisdom of Christ** and the Key of Knowledge; or, History of the Apocrypha. By ERNEST DE BUNSEN. 2 vols. 8vo. 28s.

**The Keys of St. Peter;** or, the House of Rechab, connected with the History of Symbolism and Idolatry. By the same Author. 8vo. 14s.

**The Power of the Soul over the** Body. By GEO. MOORE, M.D. M.R.C.P.L. &c. Sixth Edition. Crown 8vo. 8s. 6d.

**The Types of Genesis** briefly considered as Revealing the Development of Human Nature. By ANDREW JUKES. Second Edition. Crown 8vo. 7s. 6d.

**The Second Death and the Restitution** of All Things, with some Preliminary Remarks on the Nature and Inspiration of Holy Scripture. By the same Author. Second Edition. Crown 8vo. 3s. 6d.

**Thoughts for the Age.** BY ELIZABETH M. SEWELL, Author of 'Amy Herbert.' New Edition. Fcp. 8vo. price 5s.

**Passing Thoughts on Religion.** By the same Author. Fcp. 5s.

**Self-examination before Confirmation.** By the same Author. 32mo. 1s. 6d.

**Thoughts for the Holy Week,** for Young Persons. By the same Author. New Edition. Fcp. 8vo. 2s.

**Readings for a Month Preparatory to** Confirmation from Writers of the Early and English Church. By the same. Fcp. 4s.

**Readings for Every Day in Lent,** compiled from the Writings of Bishop JEREMY TAYLOR. By the same Author. Fcp. 5s.

**Preparation for the Holy Communion;** the Devotions chiefly from the works of JEREMY TAYLOR. By the same. 32mo. 3s.

**Principles of Education drawn from** Nature and Revelation, and Applied to Female Education in the Upper Classes. By the same Author. 2 vols. fcp. 12s. 6d.

**Bishop Jeremy Taylor's Entire** Works: with Life by BISHOP HEBER. Revised and corrected by the Rev. C. P. EDEN. 10 vols. £5 5s.

**England and Christendom.** By ARCHBISHOP MANNING, D.D. Post 8vo. price 10s. 6d.

**The Wife's Manual;** or, Prayers, Thoughts, and Songs on Several Occasions of a Matron's Life. By the Rev. W. CALVERT, M.A. Crown 8vo. 10s. 6d.

**Singers and Songs of the Church:** being Biographical Sketches of the Hymn-Writers in all the principal Collections; with Notes on their Psalms and Hymns. By JOSIAH MILLER, M.A. Second Edition, enlarged. Post 8vo. 10s. 6d.

**'Spiritual Songs' for the Sundays** and Holidays throughout the Year. By J. S. B. MONSELL, LL.D. Vicar of Egham and Rural Dean. Fourth Edition, Sixth Thousand. Fcp. price 4s. 6d.

**The Beatitudes.** By the same Author. Third Edition, revised. Fcp. 3s. 6d.

**His Presence not his Memory,** 1855. By the same Author, in memory of his SON. Sixth Edition. 16mo. 1s.

**Lyra Germanica,** translated from the German by Miss C. WINKWORTH. FIRST SERIES, the *Christian Year*, Hymns for the Sundays and Chief Festivals of the Church; SECOND SERIES, the *Christian Life*. Fcp. 8vo. price 3s. 6d. each SERIES.

**Lyra Eucharistica ;** Hymns and Verses on the Holy Communion, Ancient and Modern: with other Poems. Edited by the Rev. ORBY SHIPLEY, M.A. Second Edition. Fcp. 5s.

Shipley's **Lyra Messianica.** Fcp. 5s.

Shipley's **Lyra Mystica.** Fcp. 5s.

**Endeavours after the Christian** Life: Discourses. By JAMES MARTINEAU. Fourth Edition, carefully revised. Post 8vo. 7s. 6d.

**Invocation of Saints and Angels ;** for the use of Members of the English Church. Edited by the Rev. ORBY SHIPLEY, M.A. 24mo. 3s. 6d.

## Travels, Voyages, &c.

**The Playground of Europe.** By LESLIE STEPHEN, late President of the Alpine Club. Post 8vo. with Frontispiece. [*Just ready.*

**Westward by Rail:** the New Route to the East. By W. F. RAE. Post 8vo. with Map, price 10s. 6d.

**Travels in the Central Caucasus** and Bashan, including Visits to Ararat and Tabreez and Ascents of Kazbek and Elbruz. By DOUGLAS W. FRESHFIELD. Square crown 8vo. with Maps, &c., 18s.

**Cadore or Titian's Country.** By JOSIAH GILBERT, one of the Authors of the 'Dolomite Mountains.' With Map, Facsimile, and 40 Illustrations. Imp. 8vo. 31s. 6d.

**Zigzagging amongst Dolomites;** with more than 300 Illustrations by the Author. By the Author of 'How we Spent the Summer.' Oblong 4to. price 15s.

**The Dolomite Mountains.** Excursions through Tyrol, Carinthia, Carniola, and Friuli. By J. GILBERT and G. C. CHURCHILL, F.R.G.S. With numerous Illustrations. Square crown 8vo. 21s.

**Pilgrimages in the Pyrenees and** Landes. By DENYS SHYNE LAWLOR. Crown 8vo. with Frontispiece and Vignette, price 15s.

**How we Spent the Summer;** or, a Voyage en Zigzag in Switzerland and Tyrol with some Members of the ALPINE CLUB. Third Edition, re-drawn. In oblong 4to. with about 300 Illustrations, 15s.

**Pictures in Tyrol and Elsewhere.** From a Family Sketch-Book. By the same Author. Second Edition. 4to. with many Illustrations, 21s.

**Beaten Tracks;** or, Pen and Pencil Sketches in Italy. By the same Author. With 42 Plates of Sketches. 8vo. 16s.

**The Alpine Club Map of the Chain** of Mont Blanc, from an actual Survey in 1863 — 1864. By A. ADAMS-REILLY, F.R.G.S. M.A.C. In Chromolithography on extra stout drawing paper 28in. × 17in. price 10s. or mounted on canvas in a folding case, 12s. 6d.

**England to Delhi;** a Narrative of Indian Travel. By JOHN MATHESON, Glasgow. With Map and 82 Woodcut Illustrations. 4to. 31s. 6d.

**History of Discovery in our** Australasian Colonies, Australia, Tasmania, and New Zealand, from the Earliest Date to the Present Day. By WILLIAM HOWITT. 2 vols. 8vo. with 3 Maps, 20s.

**The Capital of the Tycoon;** a Narrative of a 3 Years' Residence in Japan. By Sir RUTHERFORD ALCOCK, K.C.B. 2 vols. 8vo. with numerous Illustrations, 42s.

**Guide to the Pyrenees,** for the use of Mountaineers. By CHARLES PACKE. Second Edition, with Maps, &c. and Appendix. Crown 8vo. 7s. 6d.

**The Alpine Guide.** By JOHN BALL, M.R.I.A. late President of the Alpine Club. Post 8vo. with Maps and other Illustrations.
Guide to the Eastern Alps, price 10s. 6d.
Guide to the Western Alps, including Mont Blanc, Monte Rosa, Zermatt, &c. price 6s. 6d.
Guide to the Central Alps, including all the Oberland District, price 7s. 6d.
Introduction on Alpine Travelling in general, and on the Geology of the Alps, price 1s. Either of the Three Volumes or Parts of the *Alpine Guide* may be had with this INTRODUCTION prefixed, price 1s. extra.

**Roma Sotterranea;** or, an Account of the Roman Catacombs, especially of the Cemetery of San Callisto. Compiled from the Works of Commendatore G. B. DE ROSSI, by the Rev. J. S. NORTHCOTE, D.D. and the Rev. W. B. BROWNLOW. With Plans and numerous other Illustrations. 8vo. 31s. 6d.

**Memorials of London and London** Life in the 13th, 14th, and 15th Centuries; being a Series of Extracts, Local, Social, and Political, from the Archives of the City of London, A.D. 1276–1419. Selected, translated, and edited by H. T. RILEY, M.A. Royal 8vo. 21s.

**Commentaries on the History,** Constitution, and Chartered Franchises of the City of London. By GEORGE NORTON, formerly one of the Common Pleaders of the City of London. Third Edition. 8vo. 14s.

**The Northern Heights of London;** or, Historical Associations of Hampstead, Highgate, Muswell Hill, Hornsey, and Islington. By WILLIAM HOWITT. With about 40 Woodcuts. Square crown 8vo. 21s.

**The Rural Life of England.** By the same Author. With Woodcuts by Bewick and Williams. Medium, 8vo. 12s. 6d.

**Visits to Remarkable Places:** Old Halls, Battle-Fields, and Scenes illustrative of striking Passages in English History and Poetry. By the same Author. 2 vols. square crown 8vo. with Wood Engravings, 25s.

**Narrative of the Euphrates Expedition** carried on by Order of the British Government during the years 1835, 1836, and 1837. By General F. R. CHESNEY, F.R.S. With 2 Maps, 45 Plates, and 16 Woodcuts. 8vo. 24s.

## Works of Fiction.

**Lothair.** By the Right Hon. B. DISRAELI, Cabinet Edition (the Eighth), complete in One Volume, with a Portrait of the Author, and a new General Preface. Crown 8vo. price 6s.—By the same Author, Cabinet Editions, revised, uniform with the above:—

| | |
|---|---|
| CONINGSBY, 6s. | ALROY; IXION; the |
| SYBIL, 6s. | INFERNAL MAR- |
| TANCRED, 6s. | RIAGE; and PO- |
| VENETIA, 6s. | PANILLA. Price 6s. |
| HENRIETTA TEMPLE, 6s. | YOUNG DUKE and COUNT ALARCOS, 6s. |
| CONTARINI FLEMING and RISE OF ISKANDER, 6s. | VIVIAN GREY, 6s. |

**The Modern Novelist's Library.** Each Work, in crown 8vo. complete in a Single Volume:—

MELVILLE'S GLADIATORS, 2s. boards; 2s. 6d. cloth.
———— GOOD FOR NOTHING, 2s. boards; 2s. 6d. cloth.
———— HOLMBY HOUSE, 2s. boards; 2s. 6d. cloth.
———— INTERPRETER, 2s. boards; 2s. 6d. cloth.
———— QUEEN'S MARIES, 2s. boards; 2s. 6d. cloth.
TROLLOPE'S WARDEN, 1s. 6d. boards; 2s. cloth.
———— BARCHESTER TOWERS, 2s. boards; 2s. 6d. cloth.
BRAMLEY-MOORE'S SIX SISTERS OF THE VALLEYS, 2s. boards; 2s. 6d. cloth.

**Stories and Tales by the Author** of 'Amy Herbert,' uniform Edition:—

| | |
|---|---|
| AMY HERBERT, 2s. 6d. | KATHARINE ASHTON, 3s. 6d. |
| GERTRUDE, 2s. 6d. | |
| EARL'S DAUGHTER, 2s. 6d. | MARGARET PERCIVAL, 5s. |
| EXPERIENCE OF LIFE, 2s. 6d. | LANETON PARSONAGE, 4s. 6d. |
| CLEVE HALL, 3s. 6d. | URSULA, 4s. 6d. |
| IVORS, 3s. 6d. | |

**A Glimpse of the World.** Fcp. 7s. 6d.
**Journal of a Home Life.** Post 8vo. 9s. 6d.
**After Life;** a Sequel to the 'Journal of a Home Life.' Post 8vo. 10s. 6d.

**A Visit to my Discontented Cousin.** Reprinted, with some Additions, from *Fraser's Magazine.* Crown 8vo. price 7s. 6d.

**Ierne;** a Tale. By W. STEUART TRENCH, Author of 'Realities of Irish Life.' 2 vols post 8vo. [*Just ready.*

**Three Weddings.** By the Author of 'Dorothy,' &c. Fcp. 8vo. 5s.

**The Giant;** a Witch's Story for English Boys. Edited by ELIZABETH M. SEWELL, Author of 'Amy Herbert,' &c. Fcp. 8vo. price 5s.

**Uncle Peter's Fairy Tale for the XIXth Century.** By the same Author and Editor. Fcp. 8vo. 7s. 6d.

**Vikram and the Vampire;** or, Tales of Hindu Devilry. Adapted by RICHARD F. BURTON, F.R.G.S. &c. With 33 Illustrations. Crown 8vo. 9s.

**Becker's Gallus;** or, Roman Scenes of the Time of Augustus. Post 8vo. 7s. 6d.

**Becker's Charicles:** Illustrative of Private Life of the Ancient Greeks. Post 8vo. 7s. 6d.

**Tales of Ancient Greece.** By GEORGE W. COX, M.A. late Scholar of Trin. Coll. Oxford. Being a collective Edition of the Author's Classical Series and Tales, complete in One Volume. Crown 8vo. 6s. 6d.

**Cabinet Edition of Novels and Tales** by G. J. WHYTE MELVILLE:—

| | |
|---|---|
| THE GLADIATORS, 5s. | HOLMBY HOUSE, 5s. |
| DIGBY GRAND, 5s. | GOOD FOR NOTHING, 6s. |
| KATE COVENTRY, 5s. | QUEEN'S MARIES, 6s. |
| GENERAL BOUNCE, 5s. | THE INTERPRETER, 5s. |

**Our Children's Story.** By One of their Gossips. By the Author of 'Voyage en Zigzag,' &c. Small 4to. with Sixty Illustrations by the Author, price 10s. 6d.

**Wonderful Stories from Norway,** Sweden, and Iceland. Adapted and arranged by JULIA GODDARD. With an Introductory Essay by the Rev. G. W. COX, M.A. and Six Illustrations. Square post 8vo. 6s.

C

## Poetry and The Drama.

**Thomas Moore's Poetical Works,** the only Editions containing the Author's last Copyright Additions:—
Shamrock Edition, price 3s. 6d.
Ruby Edition, with Portrait, 6s.
Cabinet Edition, 10 vols. fcp. 8vo. 35s.
People's Edition, Portrait, &c. 10s. 6d.
Library Edition, Portrait & Vignette, 14s.

**Moore's Lalla Rookh,** Tenniel's Edition, with 68 Wood Engravings from Original Drawings and other Illustrations. Fcp. 4to. 21s.

**Moore's Irish Melodies,** Maclise's Edition, with 161 Steel Plates from Original Drawings. Super-royal 8vo. 31s. 6d.

**Miniature Edition of Moore's Irish Melodies,** with Maclise's Illustrations (as above), reduced in Lithography. Imp. 16mo. 10s. 6d.

**Southey's Poetical Works,** with the Author's last Corrections and copyright Additions. Library Edition. Medium 8vo. with Portrait and Vignette, 14s.

**Lays of Ancient Rome;** with *Ivry* and the *Armada*. By the Right Hon. LORD MACAULAY. 16mo. 4s. 6d.

**Lord Macaulay's Lays of Ancient Rome.** With 90 Illustrations on Wood, Original and from the Antique, from Drawings by G. SCHARF. Fcp. 4to. 21s.

**Miniature Edition of Lord Macaulay's Lays of Ancient Rome,** with Scharf's Illustrations (as above) reduced in Lithography. Imp. 16mo. 10s. 6d.

**Goldsmith's Poetical Works,** Illustrated with Wood Engravings from Designs by Members of the ETCHING CLUB. Imp. 16mo. 7s. 6d.

**Poems of Bygone Years.** Edited by the Author of 'Amy Herbert.' Fcp. 8vo. 5s.

**Poems, Descriptive and Lyrical.** By THOMAS COX. New Edition. Fcp. 8vo. price 5s.

'Shew moral propriety, mental culture, and no slight acquaintance with the technicalities of song.'
ATHENÆUM.

**Madrigals, Songs, and Sonnets.** By JOHN ARTHUR BLAIKIE and EDMUND WILLIAM GOSSE. Fcp. 8vo. price 5s.

**Poems.** By JEAN INGELOW. Fifteenth Edition. Fcp. 8vo. 5s.

**Poems by Jean Ingelow.** With nearly 100 Illustrations by Eminent Artists, engraved on Wood by DALZIEL Brothers. Fcp. 4to. 21s.

**Mopsa the Fairy.** By JEAN INGELOW. With Eight Illustrations engraved on Wood. Fcp. 8vo. 6s.

**A Story of Doom,** and other Poems. By JEAN INGELOW. Third Edition. Fcp. price 5s.

**Glaphyra, and other Poems.** By FRANCIS REYNOLDS, Author of 'Alice Rushton.' 16mo. 5s.

**Bowdler's Family Shakspeare,** cheaper Genuine Edition, complete in 1 vol. large type, with 36 Woodcut Illustrations, price 14s. or in 6 pocket vols. 3s. 6d. each.

**Arundines Cami.** Collegit atque edidit H. DRURY, M.A. Editio Sexta, curavit H. J. HODGSON, M.A. Crown 8vo. price 7s. 6d.

**Horatii Opera,** Pocket Edition, with carefully corrected Text, Marginal References, and Introduction. Edited by the Rev. J. E. YONGE, M.A. Square 18mo. 4s. 6d.

**Horatii Opera,** Library Edition, with Copious English Notes, Marginal References and Various Readings. Edited by the Rev. J. E. YONGE, M.A. 8vo. 21s.

**The Æneid of Virgil** Translated into English Verse. By JOHN CONINGTON, M.A. Corpus Professor of Latin in the University of Oxford. New Edition. Crown 8vo. 9s.

**The Story of Sir Richard Whittington,** Thrice Lord Mayor of London, A.D. 1397, 1406-7, and 1419. Written in Verse and Illustrated by E. CARR. With Eleven Plates. Royal 4to. 21s.

**Hunting Songs and Miscellaneous Verses.** By R. E. EGERTON WARBURTON. Second Edition. Fcp. 8vo. 5s.

**Works by Edward Yardley:—**
FANTASTIC STORIES, fcp. 3s. 6d.
MELUSINE AND OTHER POEMS, fcp. 5s.
HORACE'S ODES TRANSLATED INTO ENGLISH VERSE, crown 8vo. 6s.
SUPPLEMENTARY STORIES AND POEMS, fcp. 3s. 6d.

## Rural Sports, &c.

**Encyclopædia of Rural Sports;** a Complete Account, Historical, Practical, and Descriptive, of Hunting, Shooting, Fishing, Racing, &c. By D. P. BLAINE. With above 600 Woodcuts (20 from Designs by JOHN LEECH). 8vo. 21s.

**The Dead Shot,** or Sportsman's Complete Guide; a Treatise on the Use of the Gun, Dog-breaking, Pigeon-shooting, &c. By MARKSMAN. Fcp. with Plates, 5s.

**A Book on Angling:** being a Complete Treatise on the Art of Angling in every branch, including full Illustrated Lists of Salmon Flies. By FRANCIS FRANCIS. Second Edition, with Portrait and 15 other Plates, plain and coloured. Post 8vo. 15s.

**Wilcocks's Sea-Fisherman:** comprising the Chief Methods of Hook and Line Fishing in the British and other Seas, a glance at Nets, and remarks on Boats and Boating. Second Edition, enlarged, with 80 Woodcuts. Post 8vo. 12s. 6d.

**The Fly-Fisher's Entomology.** By ALFRED RONALDS. With coloured Representations of the Natural and Artificial Insect. Sixth Edition, with 20 coloured Plates. 8vo. 14s.

**The Book of the Roach.** By GREVILLE FENNELL, of 'The Field.' Fcp. 8vo. price 2s. 6d.

**Blaine's Veterinary Art:** a Treatise on the Anatomy, Physiology, and Curative Treatment of the Diseases of the Horse, Neat Cattle, and Sheep. Seventh Edition, revised and enlarged by C. STEEL. 8vo. with Plates and Woodcuts, 18s.

**Horses and Stables.** By Colonel F. FITZWYGRAM, XV. the King's Hussars. Pp. 624; with 24 Plates of Illustrations, containing very numerous Figures engraved on Wood. 8vo. 15s.

**Youatt on the Horse.** Revised and enlarged by W. WATSON, M.R.C.V.S. 8vo. with numerous Woodcuts, 12s. 6d.

**Youatt on the Dog.** (By the same Author.) 8vo. with numerous Woodcuts, 6s.

**The Horse's Foot, and how to keep** it Sound. By W. MILES, Esq. Ninth Edition, with Illustrations. Imp. 8vo. 12s. 6d.

**A Plain Treatise on Horse-shoeing.** By the same Author. Sixth Edition, post 8vo. with Illustrations, 2s. 6d.

**Stables and Stable Fittings.** By the same. Imp. 8vo. with 13 Plates, 15s.

**Remarks on Horses' Teeth,** addressed to Purchasers. By the same. Post 8vo. 1s. 6d.

**Robbins's Cavalry Catechism;** or, Instructions on Cavalry Exercise and Field Movements, Brigade Movements, Out-post Duty, Cavalry supporting Artillery, Artillery attached to Cavalry. 12mo. 5s.

**The Dog in Health and Disease.** By STONEHENGE. With 70 Wood Engravings. New Edition. Square crown 8vo. 10s. 6d.

**The Greyhound.** By the same Author. Revised Edition, with 24 Portraits of Greyhounds. Square crown 8vo. 10s. 6d.

**The Ox,** his Diseases and their Treatment; with an Essay on Parturition in the Cow. By J. R. DOBSON, M.R.C.V.S. Crown 8vo. with Illustrations, 7s. 6d.

## Commerce, Navigation, and Mercantile Affairs.

**The Elements of Banking.** By HENRY DUNNING MACLEOD, M.A. of Trinity College, Cambridge, and of the Inner Temple, Barrister-at-Law. Post 8vo.
[*Nearly ready.*

**The Law of Nations Considered** as Independent Political Communities. By Sir TRAVERS TWISS, D.C.L. 2 vols. 8vo. 30s. or separately, PART I. *Peace,* 12s. PART II. *War,* 18s.

**The Theory and Practice of** Banking. By HENRY DUNNING MACLEOD, M.A. Barrister-at-Law. Second Edition. entirely remodelled. 2 vols. 8vo. 30s.

**M'Culloch's Dictionary, Prac-**tical, Theoretical, and Historical, of Commerce and Commercial Navigation. New Edition, revised throughout and corrected to the Present Time; with a Biographical Notice of the Author. Edited by H. G. REID, Secretary to Mr. M'Culloch for many years. 8vo. price 63s. cloth.

## Works of Utility and General Information.

**Modern Cookery for Private Families**, reduced to a System of Easy Practice in a Series of carefully-tested Receipts. By ELIZA ACTON. Newly revised and enlarged; with 8 Plates, Figures, and 150 Woodcuts. Fcp. 6s.

**A Practical Treatise on Brewing;** with Formulæ for Public Brewers, and Instructions for Private Families. By W. BLACK. Fifth Edition. 8vo. 10s. 6d.

**Chess Openings.** By F. W. LONGMAN, Balliol College, Oxford. Fcp. 8vo. 2s. 6d.

**The Cabinet Lawyer;** a Popular Digest of the Laws of England, Civil, Criminal, and Constitutional. 25th Edition; with Supplements of the Acts of the Parliamentary Session of 1870. Fcp. 10s. 6d.

**The Philosophy of Health;** or, an Exposition of the Physiological and Sanitary Conditions conducive to Human Longevity and Happiness. By SOUTHWOOD SMITH, M.D. Eleventh Edition, revised and enlarged; with 113 Woodcuts. 8vo. 7s. 6d.

**Maunder's Treasury of Knowledge** and Library of Reference: comprising an English Dictionary and Grammar, Universal Gazetteer, Classical Dictionary, Chronology, Law Dictionary, Synopsis of the Peerage, Useful Tables, &c. Fcp. 6s.

**Hints to Mothers on the Management** of their Health during the Period of Pregnancy and in the Lying-in Room. By T. BULL, M.D. Fcp. 5s.

**The Maternal Management of** Children in Health and Disease. By THOMAS BULL, M.D. Fcp. 5s.

**How to Nurse Sick Children;** containing Directions which may be found of service to all who have charge of the Young. By CHARLES WEST, M.D. Second Edition. Fcp. 8vo. 1s. 6d.

**Notes on Hospitals.** By FLORENCE NIGHTINGALE. Third Edition, enlarged; with 13 Plans. Post 4to. 18s.

**Pewtner's Comprehensive Specifier;** a Guide to the Practical Specification of every kind of Building-Artificer's Work: with Forms of Building Conditions and Agreements, an Appendix, Foot-Notes, and Index. Edited by W. YOUNG. Architect. Crown 8vo. 6s.

**Tidd Pratt's Law relating to** Benefit Building Societies; with Practical Observations on the Act and all the Cases decided thereon, also a Form of Rules and Forms of Mortgages. Fcp. 3s. 6d.

**Collieries and Colliers:** a Handbook of the Law and Leading Cases relating thereto. By J. C. FOWLER, of the Inner Temple, Barrister, Stipendiary Magistrate. Second Edition. Fcp. 8vo. 7s. 6d.

**Willich's Popular Tables** for Ascertaining the Value of Lifehold, Leasehold, and Church Property, Renewal Fines, &c.; the Public Funds; Annual Average Price and Interest on Consols from 1731 to 1867; Chemical, Geographical, Astronomical, Trigonometrical Tables, &c. Post 8vo. 10s.

**Coulthart's Decimal Interest** Tables at Twenty-four Different Rates not exceeding Five per Cent. Calculated for the use of Bankers. To which are added Commission Tables at One-eighth and One-fourth per Cent. 8vo. 15s.

## Periodical Publications.

**The Edinburgh Review, or Critical Journal,** published Quarterly in January, April, July, and October. 8vo. price 6s. each Number.

**Notes on Books:** An Analysis of the Works published during each Quarter by Messrs. LONGMANS & Co. The object is to enable Bookbuyers to obtain such information regarding the various works as is usually afforded by tables of contents and explanatory prefaces. 4to. Quarterly. *Gratis.*

**Fraser's Magazine.** Edited by JAMES ANTHONY FROUDE, M.A. New Series, published on the 1st of each Month. 8vo. price 2s. 6d. each Number.

**The Alpine Journal:** A Record of Mountain Adventure and Scientific Observation. By Members of the Alpine Club. Edited by LESLIE STEPHEN. Published Quarterly, May 31, Aug. 31, Nov. 30, Feb. 28. 8vo. price 1s. 6d. each No.

# INDEX.

ACTON's Modern Cookery.................. 20
ALCOCK's Residence in Japan............. 16
ALLIES on Formation of Christendom ...... 14
ALLEN's Discourses of Chrysostom ........ 14
Alpine Guide (The) ...................... 16
——— Journal ........................... 20
ALTHAUS on Medical Electricity .......... 10
ARNOLD's Manual of English Literature .. 6
ARNOTT's Elements of Physics ............ 8
Arundines Cami .......................... 18
Autumn Holidays of a Country Parson .... 6
AYRE's Treasury of Bible Knowledge...... 14

BACON's Essays by WHATELY ............. 5
——— Life and Letters, by SPEDDING .. 4
——— Works............................. 5
BAIN's Mental and Moral Science ........ 7
——— on the Emotions and Will .......... 7
——— on the Senses and Intellect ......... 7
——— on the Study of Character ......... 7
BALL's Guide to the Central Alps......... 16
———Guide to the Western Alps ........ 16
———Guide to the Eastern Alps ........ 16
BARING's Staff College Essays ............ 6
BAYLDON's Rents and Tillages ........... 13
Beaten Tracks ........................... 16
BECKER's *Charicles* and *Gallus* ........... 17
BENFEY's Sanskrit-English Dictionary .... 6
BERNARD on British Neutrality .......... 1
BERWICK's Forces of the Universe ....... 8
BLACK's Treatise on Brewing............. 20
BLACKLEY's Word-Gossip ................ 7
——————— German-English Dictionary .. 6
BLACKIE and GOSSE's Poems ............. 18
BLAINE's Rural Sports .................... 19
——— Veterinary Art ................... 19
BOURNE on Screw Propeller .............. 13
———'s Catechism of the Steam Engine.. 13
——— Examples of Modern Engines .. 13
——— Handbook of Steam Engine ... 13
——— Treatise on the Steam Engine.... 13
——— Improvements in the same ...... 13
BOWDLER's Family SHAKSPEARE......... 18
BRAMLEY-MOORE's Six Sisters of the Valley 17
BRANDE's Dictionary of Science, Literature, and Art............................... 10
BRAY's (C.) Education of the Feelings .... 7
——— Philosophy of Necessity ...... 7
——— On Force...................... 7
BROWNE's Exposition of the 39 Articles.... 13
BRUNEL's Life of BRUNEL ................ 3
BUCKLE's History of Civilisation ......... 2
BULL's Hints to Mothers.................. 20
——— Maternal Management of Children.. 20
BUNSEN's God in History................. 3
——— Memoirs ...................... 4

BUNSEN (E. De) on Apocrypha........... 15
——— 's Keys of St. Peter ............. 15
BURKE's Vicissitudes of Families .......... 4
BURTON's Christian Church ............. 3
——— Vikram and the Vampire........ 17

Cabinet Lawyer........................... 20
CALVERT's Wife's Manual ............... 15
CARR's Sir R. WHITTINGTON............. 18
CATES's Biographical Dictionary .......... 4
CATS and FARLIE's Moral Emblems .... 12
Changed Aspects of Unchanged Truths .... 6
CHESNEY's Euphrates Expedition ........ 17
——— Indian Polity ................ 2
——— Waterloo Campaign .......... 2
CHESNEY's and REEVE's Military Essays .. 2
CHILD's Physiological Essays............. 11
Chorale Book for England ............... 11
CLOUGH's Lives from Plutarch ........... 2
COLENSO (Bishop) on Pentateuch and Book of Joshua............................. 14
Commonplace Philosopher in Town and Country ............................. 6
CONINGTON's Translation of Virgil's Æneid 18
CONTANSEAU's Two French Dictionaries .. 6
CONYBEARE and HOWSON's Life and Epistles of St. Paul ........................... 13
COOPER's Surgical Dictionary............. 10
COPLAND's Dictionary of Practical Medicine 11
COTTON's (Bishop) Life................... 3
COULTHART's Decimal Interest Tables .... 20
Counsel and Comfort from a City Pulpit .. 6
Cox's (G. W.) Aryan Mythology .......... 3
——— Tale of the Great Persian War 2
——— Tales of Ancient Greece .... 17
Cox's (T.) Poems......................... 18
CRESY's Encyclopædia of Civil Engineering 13
Critical Essays of a Country Parson........ 6
CROOKES on Beet-Root Sugar............. 13
CULLEY's Handbook of Telegraphy ........ 12
CUSACK's Student's History of Ireland .... 2

D'AUBIGNÉ's History of the Reformation in the time of CALVIN .................... 2
DAVIDSON's Introduction to New Testament 14
Dead Shot (The), by MARKSMAN .......... 19
DE LA RIVE's Treatise on Electricity ...... 8
DENISON's Vice-Regal Life ............... 1
DE TOCQUEVILLE's Democracy in America. 2
DISRAELI's Lothair....................... 17
——— Novels and Tales ............. 17
DOBSON on the Ox ....................... 19
DOVE's Law of Storms ................... 8
DOYLE's Fairyland ....................... 11
DYER's City of Rome .................... 2

| | |
|---|---|
| EASTLAKE's Hints on Household Taste | 12 |
| ———— History of Oil Painting | 11 |
| ———— Life of Gibson | 11 |
| Edinburgh Review | 20 |
| EDMUNDS's Names of Places | 7 |
| Elements of Botany | 9 |
| ELLICOTT's Commentary on Ephesians | 14 |
| ———— Lectures on Life of Christ | 14 |
| ———— Commentary on Galatians | 14 |
| ———————————— Pastoral Epist. | 14 |
| ———————————— Philippians,&c. | 14 |
| ———————————— Thessalonians | 14 |
| EWALD's History of Israel | 14 |
| | |
| FAIRBAIRN's Application of Cast and Wrought Iron to Building | 12 |
| ———— Information for Engineers | 12 |
| ———— Treatise on Mills and Millwork | 12 |
| ———— Iron Shipbuilding | 12 |
| FARADAY's Life and Letters | 4 |
| FARRAR's Chapters on Language | 5 |
| ———— Families of Speech | 7 |
| FELKIN on Hosiery & Lace Manufactures | 13 |
| FENNEL's Book of the Roach | 19 |
| FFOULKES's Christendom's Divisions | 15 |
| FITZWYGRAM on Horses and Stables | 19 |
| FORBES's Earls of Granard | 4 |
| FOWLER's Collieries and Colliers | 20 |
| FRANCIS's Fishing Book | 19 |
| FRASER's Magazine | 20 |
| FRESHFIELD's Travels in the Caucasus | 16 |
| FROUDE's History of England | 1 |
| ———— Short Studies | 7 |
| | |
| GANOT's Elementary Physics | 8 |
| GIANT (The) | 17 |
| GILBERT's Cadore | 16 |
| ———— and CHURCHILL's Dolomites | 16 |
| GIRTIN's House I Live In | 11 |
| GLEDSTONE's Life of WHITEFIELD | 3 |
| GODDARD's Wonderful Stories | 17 |
| GOLDSMITH's Poems, Illustrated | 18 |
| GOULD's Silver Store | 7 |
| GRAHAM's Book About Words | 5 |
| GRANT's Ethics of Aristotle | 5 |
| ———— Home Politics | 2 |
| Graver Thoughts of a Country Parson | 6 |
| Gray's Anatomy | 11 |
| GREENHOW on Bronchitis | 10 |
| GROVE on Correlation of Physical Forces | 9 |
| GURNEY's Chapters of French History | 2 |
| GWILT's Encyclopædia of Architecture | 12 |
| | |
| HAMPDEN's (Bishop) Memorials | 3 |
| Hare on Election of Representatives | 5 |
| HARTWIG's Harmonies of Nature | 9 |
| ———— Polar World | 9 |
| ———— Sea and its Living Wonders | 9 |
| ———— Tropical World | 9 |
| HAUGHTON's Manual of Geology | 9 |
| HERSCHEL's Outlines of Astronomy | 8 |
| HEWITT on the Diseases of Women | 10 |
| HODGSON's Time and Space | 7 |
| ———— Theory of Practice | 7 |
| HOLMES's Surgical Treatment of Children | 10 |
| HOLMES's System of Surgery | 10 |
| HOOKER and WALKER-ARNOTT's British Flora | 9 |
| HORNE's Introduction to the Scriptures | 14 |
| ———— Compendium of the Scriptures | 14 |
| How we Spent the Summer | 16 |
| HOWITT's Australian Discovery | 16 |
| ———— Northern Heights of London | 16 |
| ———— Rural Life of England | 16 |
| ———— Visits to Remarkable Places | 17 |
| HÜBNER's Pope Sixtus | 3 |
| HUGHES's Manual of Geography | 8 |
| HUME's Essays | 7 |
| ———— Treatise on Human Nature | 7 |
| | |
| IHNE's History of Rome | 2 |
| INGELOW's Poems | 18 |
| ———— Story of Doom | 18 |
| ———— Mopsa | 16 |
| | |
| JAMESON's Legends of Saints and Martyrs | 12 |
| ———— Legends of the Madonna | 12 |
| ———— Legends of the Monastic Orders | 12 |
| ———— Legends of the Saviour | 12 |
| JOHNSTON's Geographical Dictionary | 8 |
| JUKES on Second Death | 15 |
| ———— on Types of Genesis | 15 |
| | |
| KALISCH's Commentary on the Bible | 5 |
| ———— Hebrew Grammar | 5 |
| KEITH on Destiny of the World | 14 |
| ———— Fulfilment of Prophecy | 14 |
| KERL's Metallurgy, by CROOKES and RÖHRIG | 13 |
| KIRBY and SPENCE's Entomology | 9 |
| | |
| LATHAM's English Dictionary | 5 |
| ———— River Plate | 8 |
| LAWLOR's Pilgrimages in the Pyrenees | 16 |
| LECKY's History of European Morals | 3 |
| ———— Rationalism | 3 |
| Leisure Hours in Town | 6 |
| Lessons of Middle Age | 6 |
| LEWES's Biographical History of Philosophy | 3 |
| LEWIS's Letters | 4 |
| LIDDELL and SCOTT's Greek-English Lexicon | 6 |
| ———— Abridged ditto | 6 |
| Life of Man Symbolised | 12 |
| ———— Margaret M. Hallahan | 14 |
| LINDLEY and MOORE's Treasury of Botany | 9 |
| LINDSAY's Evidence for the Papacy | 14 |
| LONGMAN's Edward the Third | 2 |
| ———— Lectures on History of England | 2 |
| ———— Chess Openings | 20 |
| Lord's Prayer Illustrated | 11 |
| LOUDON's Encyclopædia of Agriculture | 13 |
| ———— Gardening | 13 |
| ———— Plants | 9 |
| LOWNDES's Engineer's Handbook | 12 |
| LUBBOCK's Origin of Civilisation | 9 |
| Lyra Eucharistica | 15 |
| ———— Germanica | 11, 15 |
| ———— Messianica | 15 |

| | |
|---|---|
| Lyra Mystica | 15 |
| MACAULAY'S (Lord) Essays | 3 |
| ———— History of England | 1 |
| ———— Lays of Ancient Rome | 18 |
| ———— Miscellaneous Writings | 7 |
| ———— Speeches | 5 |
| ———— Works | 1 |
| MACFARREN'S Lectures on Harmony | 11 |
| MACLEOD'S Elements of Political Economy | 5 |
| ———— Dictionary of Political Economy | 5 |
| ———— Elements of Banking | 19 |
| ———— Theory and Practice of Banking | 19 |
| MCCULLOCH'S Dictionary of Commerce | 19 |
| ———— Geographical Dictionary | 8 |
| MAGUIRE'S Life of Father Mathew | 4 |
| ———— PIUS IX | 14 |
| MALET'S Overthrow of Germanic Confederation | 2 |
| MANNING'S England and Christendom | 15 |
| MARCET on the Larynx | 11 |
| MARSHALL'S Physiology | 11 |
| MARSHMAN'S History of India | 2 |
| ———— Life of Havelock | 4 |
| MARTINEAU'S Endeavours after the Christian Life | 15 |
| MASSINGBERD'S History of the Reformation | 3 |
| MATHESON'S England to Delhi | 16 |
| MAUNDER'S Biographical Treasury | 4 |
| ———— Geographical Treasury | 8 |
| ———— Historical Treasury | 3 |
| ———— Scientific and Literary Treasury | 20 |
| ———— Treasury of Knowledge | 4 |
| ———— Treasury of Natural History | 9 |
| MAY'S Constitutional History of England | 1 |
| MELVILLE'S Digby Grand | 17 |
| ———— General Bounce | 17 |
| ———— Gladiators | 17 |
| ———— Good for Nothing | 17 |
| ———— Holmby House | 17 |
| ———— Interpreter | 17 |
| ———— Kate Coventry | 17 |
| ———— Queen's Maries | 17 |
| MENDELSSOHN'S Letters | 4 |
| MERIVALE'S Fall of the Roman Republic | 2 |
| ———— Romans under the Empire | 2 |
| MERRIFIELD and EVERS'S Navigation | 8 |
| MILES on Horse's Foot and Horse Shoeing | 19 |
| ———— on Horses' Teeth and Stables | 19 |
| MILL (J.) on the Mind | 5 |
| MILL (J. S.) on Liberty | 4 |
| ———— Subjection of Women | 4 |
| ———— on Representative Government | 4 |
| ———— on Utilitarianism | 4 |
| ———— 's Dissertations and Discussions | 4 |
| ———— Political Economy | 4 |
| MILL'S System of Logic | 5 |
| ———— Hamilton's Philosophy | 4 |
| ———— Inaugural Address at St. Andrew's | 4 |
| MILLER'S Elements of Chemistry | 10 |
| ———— Hymn Writers | 15 |
| MITCHELL'S Manual of Architecture | 12 |
| ———— Manual of Assaying | 13 |
| MONSELL'S Beatitudes | 15 |
| ———— His Presence not his Memory | 15 |
| ———— 'Spiritual Songs' | 15 |
| MOORE'S Irish Melodies | 18 |
| ———— Lalla Rookh | 18 |
| ———— Journal and Correspondence | 3 |
| ———— Poetical Works | 18 |
| ———— (Dr. G.) Power of the Soul over the Body | 15 |
| MORELL'S Elements of Psychology | 7 |
| MORELL'S Mental Philosophy | 7 |
| MÜLLER'S (Max) Chips from a German Workshop | 7 |
| ———— Lectures on the Science of Language | 5 |
| ———— (K. O.) Literature of Ancient Greece | 2 |
| MURCHISON on Liver Complaints | 11 |
| MURE'S Language and Literature of Greece | 2 |
| | |
| New Testament Illustrated with Wood Engravings from the Old Masters | 12 |
| NEWMAN'S History of his Religious Opinions | 4 |
| NIGHTINGALE'S Notes on Hospitals | 20 |
| NILSSON'S Scandinavia | 9 |
| NORTHCOTE'S Sanctuary of the Madonna | 14 |
| NORTHCOTT on Lathes and Turning | 12 |
| NORTON'S City of London | 16 |
| Notes on Books | 20 |
| | |
| ODLING'S Animal Chemistry | 10 |
| ———— Course of Practical Chemistry | 10 |
| ———— Manual of Chemistry | 10 |
| ———— Lectures on Carbon | 10 |
| ———— Outlines of Chemistry | 10 |
| O'FLANAGAN'S Irish Chancellors | 4 |
| Our Children's Story | 17 |
| OWEN'S Comparative Anatomy and Physiology of Vertebrate Animals | 9 |
| ———— Lectures on the Invertebrata | 9 |
| | |
| PACKE'S Guide to the Pyrenees | 16 |
| PAGET'S Lectures on Surgical Pathology | 10 |
| PEREIRA'S Manual of Materia Medica | 11 |
| PERKINS'S Italian and Tuscan Sculptors | 12 |
| PEWTNER'S Comprehensive Specifier | 20 |
| Pictures in Tyrol | 16 |
| PIESSE'S Art of Perfumery | 13 |
| ———— Chemical, Natural, and Physical Magic | 13 |
| PONTON'S Beginning | 9 |
| PRATT'S Law of Building Societies | 20 |
| PRENDERGAST'S Mastery of Languages | 6 |
| PRESCOTT'S Scripture Difficulties | 14 |
| Present-Day Thoughts, by A. K. H. B. | 6 |
| PROCTOR'S Handbook of the Stars | 8 |
| ———— Saturn | 8 |
| ———— Other Worlds than Ours | 8 |
| ———— Sun | 8 |
| | |
| RAE'S Westward by Rail | 16 |
| Recreations of a Country Parson | 6 |
| REICHEL'S See of Rome | 14 |
| REILLY'S Map of Mont Blanc | 16 |
| REIMANN on Aniline Dyes | 13 |
| REYNOLDS'S Glaphyra | 18 |
| RILEY'S Memorials of London | 16 |
| RIVERS'S Rose Amateur's Guide | 9 |
| ROBBINS'S Cavalry Catechism | 19 |
| ROGERS'S Correspondence of Greyson | 7 |
| ———— Eclipse of Faith | 7 |
| ———— Defence of Faith | 7 |
| ROGET'S Thesaurus of English Words and Phrases | 5 |
| Roma Sotterranea | 16 |

| | |
|---|---|
| RONALDS's Fly-Fisher's Entomology | 19 |
| ROSE's Loyola | 14 |
| ROTHSCHILD's Israelites | 14 |
| ROWTON's Debater | 5 |
| RULE's Karaite Jews | 14 |
| RUSSELL on Government and Constitution | 1 |
| ———'s (Earl) Speeches and Despatches | 1 |
| | |
| SANDARS's Justinian's Institutes | 5 |
| SCOTT's Lectures on the Fine Arts | 11 |
| ——— Albert Durer | 11 |
| SEEBOHM's Oxford Reformers of 1498 | 2 |
| SEWELL's After Life | 17 |
| ——— Glimpse of the World | 17 |
| ——— History of the Early Church | 3 |
| ——— Journal of a Home Life | 17 |
| ——— Passing Thoughts on Religion | 15 |
| ——— Poems of Bygone Years | 18 |
| ——— Preparation for Communion | 15 |
| ——— Principles of Education | 15 |
| ——— Readings for Confirmation | 15 |
| ——— Readings for Lent | 15 |
| ——— Examination for Confirmation | 15 |
| ——— Stories and Tales | 17 |
| ——— Thoughts for the Age | 15 |
| ——— Thoughts for the Holy Week | 15 |
| SHAKSPEARE's Midsummer Night's Dream, illustrated with Silhouettes | 12 |
| SHIPLEY's Four Cardinal Virtues | 14 |
| ——— Invocation of Saints | 15 |
| SHORT's Church History | 3 |
| Smart's WALKER's English Dictionaries | 5 |
| SMITH's (SOUTHWOOD) Philosophy of Health | 20 |
| ——— (J.) Paul's Voyage and Shipwreck | 14 |
| ——— (SYDNEY) Life and Letters | 3 |
| ——— Miscellaneous Works | 7 |
| ——— Wit and Wisdom | 7 |
| SOUTHEY's Doctor | 5 |
| ——— Poetical Works | 18 |
| STANLEY's History of British Birds | 9 |
| STEBBING's Analysis of MILL's Logic | 5 |
| STEPHEN's Ecclesiastical Biography | 4 |
| ——— Playground of Europe | 16 |
| STIRLING's Secret of Hegel | 7 |
| ——— Sir WILLIAM HAMILTON | 7 |
| STONEHENGE on the Dog | 19 |
| ——— on the Greyhound | 19 |
| STRICKLAND's Tudor Princesses | 4 |
| ——— Queens of England | 4 |
| Strong and Free | 7 |
| Sunday Afternoons at the Parish Church of a Scottish University City | 6 |
| | |
| TAYLOR's History of India | 2 |
| ——— (Jeremy) Works, edited by EDEN | 15 |
| THIRLWALL's History of Greece | 2 |
| THOMSON's Conspectus | 11 |
| ——— Laws of Thought | 5 |
| Three Weddings | 17 |

| | |
|---|---|
| TODD (A.) on Parliamentary Government | 1 |
| ——— and BOWMAN's Anatomy and Physiology of Man | 11 |
| TRENCH's Ierne | 17 |
| ——— Realities of Irish Life | 2 |
| TROLLOPE's Barchester Towers | 17 |
| ——— Warden | 17 |
| TWISS's Law of Nations | 19 |
| TYNDALL's Diamagnetism | 8 |
| ——— Faraday as a Discoverer | 4 |
| ——— Lectures on Electricity | 9 |
| ——— Lectures on Light | 8 |
| ——— Lectures on Sound | 8 |
| ——— Heat a Mode of Motion | 8 |
| ——— Essays on the Imagination in Science | 9 |
| Uncle PETER's Fairy Tale | 18 |
| URE's Dictionary of Arts, Manufactures, and Mines | 12 |
| | |
| VAN DER HOEVEN's Handbook of Zoology | 9 |
| Visit to my Discontented Cousin | 17 |
| | |
| WARBURTON's Hunting Songs | 18 |
| WATSON's Principles and Practice of Physic | 10 |
| WATTS's Dictionary of Chemistry | 10 |
| WEBB's Objects for Common Telescopes | 8 |
| WEBSTER & WILKINSON's Greek Testament | 14 |
| WELLINGTON's Life, by GLEIG | 4 |
| WEST on Children's Diseases | 10 |
| ——— on Nursing Children | 20 |
| WHATELY's English Synonymes | 5 |
| ——— Logic | 5 |
| ——— Rhetoric | 5 |
| WHITE and RIDDLE's Latin Dictionaries | 6 |
| WILCOCKS's Sea Fisherman | 19 |
| WILLIAMS's Aristotle's Ethics | 5 |
| ——— History of Wales | 1 |
| WILLIAMS on Climate of South of France | 10 |
| ——— Consumption | 11 |
| WILLICH's Popular Tables | 20 |
| WILLIS's Principles of Mechanism | 12 |
| WINSLOW on Light | 8 |
| WOOD's (J. G.) Bible Animals | 9 |
| ——— Homes without Hands | 9 |
| ——— (T.) Chemical Notes | 10 |
| WOODWARD and CATER's Encyclopædia | 3 |
| | |
| YARDLEY's Poetical Works | 18 |
| YONGE's History of England | 1 |
| ——— English-Greek Lexicons | 6 |
| ——— Two Editions of Horace | 18 |
| YOUATT on the Dog | 19 |
| ——— on the Horse | 19 |
| | |
| ZELLER's Socrates | 3 |
| ——— Stoics, Epicureans, and Sceptics | 3 |
| Zigzagging amongst Dolomites | 16 |

www.ingramcontent.com/pod-product-compliance
Lightning Source LLC
Chambersburg PA
CBHW020254170426

43202CB00008B/366